Small Store Success

Small Store Success

All of the necessary ingredients for starting and operating your own store:

- ☐ Store layout & design
- ☐ Promotions
- ☐ Advertising
- ☐ Planning new seasons
- ☐ Buying merchandise
- ☐ Controlling inventory
- ☐ Catering to customers
- ☐ Much, much, more!

Ruth Pittman

BOB ADAMS, INC.
PUBLISHERS
Holbrook, Massachusetts

Published by
Bob Adams, Inc.
260 Center Street
Holbrook, Massachusetts 02343

ISBN: 1-55850-940-2

Printed in the United States of America

10 9 8 7 6 5 4 3 2 1

CONTENTS

Introduction

Section I: Your store/15

Section II: Keeping records/35

Section III: Promotions/49

Section IV: Doing your own advertising/71

To Frank, the best research assistant in the land.

INTRODUCTION

ABOUT THIS BOOK

Retailing is one of the most exciting business areas you can enter. If you have dreamed of opening up (or increasing sales in) your own small store, this book will offer invaluable advice on such topics as store design and layout, inventory control, advertising, employee relations, and many more.

Each issue is keyed to a single chapter within the book's main sections. You may wish to highlight chapters of interest to you and consult them first; or you may find it most effective to proceed through the book in the order presented, returning later to review important sections.

Because it is of interest to so many of the small store operators likely to read this book, the retail apparel sector is highlighted in a number of the chapters. You will find, however, even if your store does not sell clothing or fashion accessories, that most of the ideas outlined here can be easily adapted to your business.

RP

SECTION I:
YOUR STORE

Chapter One:
TURNING DREAMS
INTO REALITY

Do you have a dream you've cherished for years, a dream of running your own retail store? Or maybe you dream of taking some dramatic step that will make the store you already have more exciting and profitable. You've thought about this new venture for so long that you're sure you've considered every aspect of its success or failure. If that's the case, the time for dreaming is past and the time for action at hand.

The first thing you must do is put your dream to the test: Run through a feasibility checklist to determine if the idea stands a chance. A feasibility check asks questions about your new venture to provide the answer to the biggest question: Should I take this step?

You'll need to examine your willingness to work hard, your ability to get along with other people, and your readiness to put your life savings at risk. Some of the questions will explore your skills, your understanding of the business you want to open, and what you see as the need for the goods you want to sell.

Some entrepreneurs spend a great deal of money hiring experts to perform feasibility studies, but you can do it yourself with the help of Small Business Administration (SBA) management aid, number 2.026, "Feasibility Checklist for Starting a Small Business." For about a dollar you can get a copy of the leaflet from SBA; P.O. Box 15434; Fort Worth, TX 76119.

You may also want to call the nearest office of the SBA (listed in the federal government white pages of your phone book) and ask for a start-up kit. That little clutch of pamphlets describes the SBA's loan program, explains its other services, offers advice on taxes and licenses and lists helpful brochures and booklets that address almost every problem a small business owner can encounter. The kit is free.

In a recent article in the *Los Angeles Times*, William A. Cohen, professor of marketing at California State University, Los Angeles, advises anyone considering starting a new venture to "write a plan for yourself, even if you can't afford to pay a consultant to do one for you." Cohen, who is also head of his school's Small Business Institute (a service in cooperation with the Small Business

Administration) advises you to put everything on paper. Show your goals, what resources you'll need to reach them, where to get funding. "To get a loan of any kind," Cohen points out, "you'll need the plan, anyway." You can get help in formulating that plan from the SBA's management aid "Business Plan for Retailers" (number 2.020), available in many government bookstores or by mail from the Fort Worth address. It, too, will cost about $1.00.

The business plan should help you determine how much you'll have to spend on rent, utilities, taxes, license fees, insurance, and so on. It will show you how to decide where to advertise and how much you'll need to spend. One important item that many overlook in launching a new venture is profit, the income you'll need to support yourself and your family. You'll want to work out early in your planning the absolute minimum you need to survive. A well-run retail operation should show a net profit of 10 to 14 percent. Can the merchandise you want to sell support your family at that excellent profit level? How will you live if you don't make that kind of return? All these are aspects of a business that you must have firmly in mind before you commit yourself to the venture.

If all your preliminary work shows that the store you dream of has a chance of success, that you have the necessary management ability to run it, that you can learn from your mistakes before it's too late, you'll want to look into where you should locate your store.

The location you choose may be one of the most important of all the decisions you'll be making as you get started. A bad choice can almost guarantee failure of your store, while a good choice may assure success.

The first step in making this choice is influenced by your personal tastes. You'll want to locate your business in a neighborhood you like and feel comfortable in, even one where you'd like to live. It's probable that you'll like the kind of people who live in an area you find attractive, and it's vital to your store's success that you like its potential customers.

The importance of your decision on location becomes apparent when you consider that women (who do most of the shopping in this country) rate convenience of location second only to quality and service when they select a store at which to shop. Another factor that will affect your site selection is the merchandise you plan to sell. Consumers tend to divide retail goods into three types: convenience, shopping, and specialty. Convenience goods usually sell for low unit prices and are bought often. It's merchandise customers want to buy with as little effort as possible and often buy on impulse. Good examples of convenience goods are candy bars, cigarettes and milk. Stores selling this type of goods should be in an easily accessible area of heavy traffic, where passing shoppers will be reminded that they want or need the items on display. Mini-malls are often good sites since they are usually adjacent to residential areas.

Shopping goods are items that consumers buy less frequently and require a more intensive selling effort on the part of the store owner. Examples are furniture, men's suits, and automobiles. Most consumers comparison shop when they buy this higher-priced merchandise, so stores selling it should be situated close to traffic generators, such as department stores, or in shopping centers.

Specialty goods usually sell for higher unit prices, are bought less often, and are often presold because of brands. Some examples are expensive jewelry and perfume, furs, and upscale apparel. Stores that sell specialty goods usually do best when located near other specialty stores. Large malls and shopping centers are often home to hosts of specialty stores.

Once you've defined the type of area you seek, you'll need to learn as much as possible about any site you're considering. How many people live in the trading area? What is their average income? How much foot traffic passes the location you're considering? Is there plenty of parking space? Walk around the mall or shopping center you're interested in. Do the shoppers appear to be likely customers for the goods you plan to sell? Are there already several stores that will compete with yours? Will their competition stimulate business or divide it up too thinly? Talk to store owners to learn if the area is generally thriving. No amount of demographic studies will take the place of your own personal observations.

Find out if there's a merchants' association in each mall or area you're considering. Such a group can be effective in dealing with city planners and planning holiday promotions. Many merchants' associations offer group advertising, insurance, and security measures. Ask owners of other stores in the area if the association is effective, who its officers are, how often it meets, how much yearly dues are, and what it has accomplished in the past year or so.

Usually if there is no merchants' group, the shopping area will be run down and untidy and have many vacant stores, as well as a parking lot in need of repairs. Don't let yourself be fooled into believing that your enthusiasm and exciting merchandise or the promise of low rent can overcome the disadvantages of such depressed areas.

You'll need to find out about rents, of course, and whether a prospective landlord is responsive to tenants' needs and willing to invest in keeping his property in good shape. Often a landlord can be a significant factor in the success or failure of a business, so you'll want to talk to current and former tenants of any store you're considering. Ask them if the landlord returns phone calls, if he or she sends service people promptly when asked and does more for tenants than just collecting rents.

The SBA has another excellent management aid, "Choosing a Retail Location" (number 2.021), that can be most helpful to you in making this decision. The publication may be available at a government bookstore, or you can order a copy by mail from the Fort Worth address cited earlier. You may find it easier--and certainly faster--to borrow it from a public library that is designated a "government depository." Such libraries have collections of government publications that you can photocopy or even take home for two weeks or more. You can find one of the almost 2,000 depository libraries by calling the libraries in your area. Be sure to ask if their collection includes SBA publications, since no single library could possibly have room for all the tons of paper the government turns out each year.

Another source of help in choosing a site for your store might be a private organization such as Urban Decision Systems, Inc. (UDS) of Los Angeles and Westport, Connecticut. This firm advertises that they provide "tools for successful market planning," and samples of their product seem to testify to the truth of their claims. For a relatively modest $75, they'll provide you with a demographic study of a three-mile area around a site you're considering. That study will tell you about the population, number of households and families, the ethnic make-up of that population, its age and income, and the number of families that own the houses they occupy. Of course, you can spend much more and learn much more about even larger areas. Just call (800) 633-9568 (in California: (213) 820-8931) and ask to speak to a marketing representative. That person will help you decide what it is you need to know and arrange for you to receive your report in just a few days. It won't cost you a dime to look into using one of these firms and you may be pleasantly surprised at how little you'll have to spend for help in making one of the most important decisions of your business venture.

Read chapter 51 of this book carefully, too. It offers you a host of free and low-cost help from the SBA. Watch your daily papers for announcements of meetings and seminars for small business managers and read as many business publications as you can find time for. There are scores of people out there waiting to help you in person and in print; let them show you how to make a success of your new venture.

Chapter Two:
LESS IS MORE . . .
EFFECTIVE

The woman who has to look good all the time has almost no time to spend looking. She wants to buy her clothing at a store where she can find exactly what she needs, without spending hours shoving the wrong sizes and colors around a rack while she searches for the right ones. Thus, for a clothing store, the need is obvious for displays that reveal quickly and effortlessly to your customer what's in your store that will complement her existing wardrobe or help her create a new one.

What do fan-fold panels, gym rings, and exposed lath strips have to do with how you can meet the needs of these busy and demanding customers? Those devices are just some of the innovative means trend-setting retail stores are using to create appealing displays that urge shoppers to look, linger, and buy. Gone are the huge rounders with hundreds of garments crammed between size markers and topped with gaudy SALE! placards. Gone, too, from many stores, are stilted mannequins posturing grotesquely to demonstrate fullness of skirt or cut of jacket. In place of those old-fashioned, space filling fixtures are spare selections of garments displayed so customers can see what you have and buy what they like.

At Henri Bendel, the New York specialty store with a wonderful sense of what's fresh and alive, sweaters are hung on a rack, but only one of each that the store offers. When the shopper sees a style she likes, she asks for her size in the color she wants. Bendel has solved the problem of bleak racks of limp swimsuits, too. A single example of each suit is displayed on fan-fold panels, similar to those in fabric or wallpaper showrooms. Dresses are grouped together, and so are skirts, coats, and jackets, all set out in wide-open spaces. "Women want to be able to see it all first," says Geraldine Stutz, Bendels president, "and then make choices."

American High, an active sportswear boutique (also in New York City), hangs its brightly colored jumpsuits, t-shirts, and sweat pants from rings, ropes, and a blackboard. While the gymnasium effect is a far cry from the elegance of Bendel's displays, the principle remains the same: Show one of everything, and let the shopper choose from what she sees.

One of the most effective means of display--and the one that is the least costly to install--is three or four horizontal lath strips running along the wall, like a musical staff, with merchandise hung at different levels in the manner of the notes of a score. Mounted with spacers so they're not quite flat against the wall, the wood strips support hangers bearing components of complete outfits, collections of sweaters or blouses, or a variety of garments. Ingenious lighting can spotlight individual items or make the wall display the focal point of a particular area.

A popular and successful variation on the horizontal strip is wall display panels, solid or pegboard. A single item or an entire collection can be dramatically displayed without taking up even one inch of floor space. Such wall displays have the added advantage that they are easy to change, as well as attractive and space saving. In just a few minutes you can give your store a fresh look by hanging a couple of new arrivals on the lath strips or pinning a new outfit to the wall panel.

At Charivari, another of New York's forward-looking specialty stores, the lath-stripped wall display serves a dual purpose. With only six or seven garments hanging on its nearly 25-foot length, the horizontal lines draw shoppers to the back of the store where a smoked plexiglass three-tiered "counter" is suspended from the ceiling by almost invisible cords. On the shelves of that floating display are hats, belts, accessories of every type, but just one of each.

Luring shoppers to the rear of the store can be a real challenge, one that many merchandisers fail to meet because they crowd the area near the door with racks that make passage to the back uninviting or difficult. At Irresistibles in the Stamford (Connecticut) Town Center mall, white lacquered cubes angle along the floor on both sides of the entrance, forming a funnel that draws shoppers to the main display area at the rear of the store. Atop each cube is a single scarf, belt, handbag, or other accessory.

The angling technique is used by many retailers in an effort to slide the customer further into their stores. Some even have slanted store fronts that push shoppers to the center of the store when they pass the doorway. Such structural devices aren't always possible, of course, but a counter can be used to create the same effect.

Ice, in the Beverly Center mall in Los Angeles, uses its floor to conquer the problem of enticing shoppers through the entire store. Pale carpet is laid on both sides of the door, leaving the soft blue tile floor exposed in an off-center aisle that leads straight to an inviting seating arrangement complete with handsome plants and a coffee pot. The aisle is flanked on the one hand by a case displaying jewelry and on the other by widely spaced groupings of clothing.

Lillie Rubin in New York City features a seating area, too. It's a square one in the center of the front portion of the store, providing a convenient viewing site for garment displays that line the walls. It's an attractive, comfortable arrangement, but it seems to discourage shoppers from wandering to the rear of the store where costume jewelry and accessories are on display.

It's not quite clear whether seating areas represent your store's most profitable use of space. In most malls, ample seating space is provided in the concourses and the opportunity to rest her feet won't necessarily lure a shopper into a store. On the other hand, when shopping along a city street, the customer may regard as a haven any store that offers her the opportunity to relax for a few moments. What is clear, however, is that if you succeed in enticing shoppers to penetrate further into your store's interior and linger there, you'll find your sales on the increase.

Window displays that are uncluttered and attractive will serve notice to passers-by that your store is innovative and easy to shop in. Many stores accomplish the lean, clean look by using flat wooden figures with hinged joints in lieu of lifelike mannequins. In one particularly attractive window display in Beverly Center, the arms of two figures point to the interior of the store, in an all but irresistible gesture of invitation.

Controlled sparseness, then, is the look to strive for. Even though shopping is no longer an entertainment for most women, it can be relaxing if the customer isn't assaulted with hundreds of garments in a clutter that destroys her enthusiasm. A few jaunty wall displays and generic groupings of clothing in wide-open spaces will give your store a high-class, understated look that will tell your customers they're in a store that recognizes their needs.

Chapter Three:
HOW TO USE COLOR

The purpose of your store's color scheme is to attract the eye of potential customers and create a pleasing environment for the sale of merchandise. Thus, the colors you use should appeal to the average taste and be bright and clean in tone. Avoid both drabness and extreme high style if you want to evoke favorable responses. Use a variety of colors, too, colors that command attention and have mass appeal.

A store that is well coordinated in its use of color appeals to the taste of the public. Any experienced retailer knows that the right colors of merchandise sell in profitable volume while the wrong colors gather dust on the shelves. In store decoration, good colors invite traffic and draw shoppers away from the competition. If your store looks drab, if it's too old or too high fashion, potential customers will turn away and look elsewhere.

Customers are no different in their attitude toward the general atmosphere of a store than they are to the things the store sells. If a customer wouldn't buy purplish mauve or mustard yellow garments, she probably wouldn't shop in a store decorated in those colors. Subconsciously a woman may not expect to find pleasing apparel in a store decorated in colors she dislikes. Hence, you need to decorate with colors that have been proven to appeal to most people.

The most liked colors are blue, red, green, and yellow. Thus, these hues (and tints of them) are good colors for walls, fixtures, and displays. They are universally enjoyed by persons of all ethnic backgrounds and age levels. Robert Ridgway, in his book *Color*, recommends bright and pastel shades of peacock, canary, emerald, pink, and blue, along with pastel orange and lime green as the best sprightly colors for store decoration. He adds forest green, walnut brown, maroon, and marine blue as the four dark colors that will appeal to most shoppers. He points out that while white holds little appeal in itself, it is clean looking and never clashes with other colors. However, he warns, large expanses of white can draw shoppers' eyes away from the merchandise on display.

Generally speaking, the pastel colors Ridgway names should be used on upper walls, while the bright colors are recommended for backgrounds and displays in a direct line with the customers' vision. Deep colors should be used to supply accents.

How much color should you use and how many different ones? That will depend on circumstances and the class of trade you hope to attract. A shop catering to an exclusive clientele can be quite unusual, choosing colors according to the taste of the owner. A store that caters to the average public, however, should shun overstyling in favor of frank and honest good taste.

Many stores make a practice of using a light color--generally an off-white--as a major theme, then contrasting it with brighter hues. For example, pastel and bright peacock are highly recommended for women's wear, since this hue is the direct complement of the human complexion. A woman trying on a dress amid shades of peacock will see her mirror image at its very best. Emerald and pink are good colors for women's shops, also. Cool colors should be used in hot climates and warm colors where the weather is generally cold.

You'll want to avoid too much brilliant color, however. Use it to direct the eye to locations where selling is done. Intense colors like pastel orange and lime green can be spotted at the far ends of stores to attract customers toward those areas.

The deep tones should be reserved for areas directly in back of merchandise, not used on upper walls or wide expanses. These darker colors will create an effective contrast with merchandise, setting it off dramatically. Fixtures, tables, and counters should usually be in neutral tones of sand, beige, or warm gray. In other words, use a bright color to bring customers to the products, then let the fixture be light in tone for a local contrast.

Study the color schemes of other apparel stores. If cash registers are jingling and customers look content, those color schemes must be deemed successful. For example, a flourishing lingerie shop in Arizona uses a color scheme of pink and beige to set off the usually subtle colors of its merchandise. A Nevada women's store features soft tan walls and a beige floor striped with yellow and brown. Contrast is supplied by wall designs in gold and bright red. These stores are designed to suit their climates, merchandise, and customers. You can accomplish the same ends by designing a color scheme that showcases your merchandise, appeals to your customers, and makes your store more inviting than others in the neighborhood.

Chapter Four:
LIGHTING FOR SUCCESS

Without an effective lighting scheme, even the most attractively decorated store can fail to attract customers. Brightness attracts while dimness may be passed by; brightness stimulates emotional response and prompts actions. But light used improperly can create a cold and forbidding atmosphere. A well-lit appearance stemming from medium levels of light helps to promote a sense of well being, the feeling you hope to inspire in every shopper who crosses your threshold.

Achieving that good lighting effect isn't easy, however, since the rules of lighting are riddled with apparent contradictions. A room in which little or no light reaches the ceiling may appear gloomy, while a room with light spilling upward to the ceiling may seem to be well lit even with a reduced illumination level. Too little light may inhibit action on the part of your customers; too much light can have the same effect. A great deal of bright light distracts attention from the goods you want to sell, and glare makes shoppers uncomfortable. A store lighted to an overall high intensity may not appear to be as well lit as one with half the amount of light but with bright points that give sparkle.

Apparel stores are particularly in need of good lighting because it's so important for customers to see themselves and what they buy in the best light. Some experts say no apparel store would remain in business if it were lit with natural light alone, since the colors of goods displayed would often be distorted. Natural light should be restricted in apparel stores and replaced with warm light that flatters the complexion yet gives an impression of daylight.

Both direct and indirect lighting should be combined for best effect. Direct light creates appealing contrasts of light and dark. Used incorrectly, however, direct light causes uncomfortable glare. Indirect (or diffused) light must also be used judiciously, since used alone it can make customers drowsy.

Light fixtures can be fastened directly to ceiling or walls, suspended on short or long stems down from the ceiling or out from the walls. Ceiling fixtures can be recessed or concealed behind slats, luminous panels, or egg-crate louvers; wall light fixtures can be hidden by colored uprights to create a mural effect that will attract shoppers toward it. Luminous walls make good screens for light sources, too, providing different effects depending on the number and position of fixtures behind them.

What type of light should you choose for your store? Incandescent light is popular because it's warm and builds highlights and shadows. Fluorescent tubes, however, will cost about four times as much as ordinary incandescent lights, but will cost about one-tenth as much to operate. Daylight fluorescent tubes, with a high proportion of blue light, are unkind to human skin tones and aren't recommended. Deluxe tubes in both cool and warm white are a little more expensive to operate than the daylight variety, but unquestionably provide the best lighting for making colors look good. They create a friendly ambiance, lending warmth to merchandise, customers, and staff.

Fred Macarai, instructor of lighting design in the University of California at Los Angeles extension program, says you can get help with your lighting problems from vendors of lighting fixtures, electrical contractors, electrical engineers, or lighting designers. However, Macarai points out, nonprofessionals with a little imagination can apply their own tricks.

A simple fluorescent tube will create a special mood if it's sheathed in a colored tube guard. Picture-frame lights installed around a wall grouping or beneath a small counter create a special display. Direct recessed light focused through a smaller-than-usual opening will create a pool of light on an important area. A specially cut opening placed on the front of a track light creates an unusual beam of light to highlight a garment or collection.

With a little bit of research and imagination you can arrange your store's lighting so that customers will feel attractive and your merchandise will look its best in a warm and friendly atmosphere.

Chapter Five:
MAKING SCENES

Every day hundreds--if not thousands--of people stream past your store windows, a small fraction of them stopping to look at what you've created there. If your displays--window or in-store--are cluttered or dull, you're missing a chance to attract attention and reinforce your store image.

Displays should not be just arrays of goods, says Barry James Wood, author of *Show Windows: 75 Years of the Art of Display*. "One has only to note the crowds that gather around any window display of striking originality to realize how eagerly the populace responds to any change. . . ."

"The reason for display," says Candy Pratts, one of New York's outstanding display artists, "is not to sell but to entertain and attract. After all," she goes on, "you can buy a Klein, Lauren, or Saint Laurent dress in half a dozen stores around town. What brings the customer to a particular store is the image the window sells." Bob Mahoney, display designer for Gumps, says the purpose of window displays is to get the passerby's attention for two seconds--and to tantalize that person into the store. "If you can't stop 'em, you can't sell 'em," he explains, adding that he prides himself on creating displays on a low budget.

Limited budgets demand the utmost in ingenuity. Always be on the lookout for free or inexpensive props. When you visit the seashore, for example, collect unusual pieces of driftwood, shells, even a bucket of beautiful white sand. The cardboard tubes that fabrics are rolled on can easily be made into rockets for a July 4 display, say, or red-and-white striped poles for a Christmas setting. Keep a supply of lace paper doilies, crepe paper, bricks, old shutters, and black tape to use in creating illusions. Use materials at hand and your imagination to create a scene; set the stage for merchandise you're featuring. Display artist Jim Buckley says, "Improvisation is the core of display vitality." So let your imagination run free. Use hearts at Valentine's Day, but not red ones; create a giant chess board and position merchandise on the squares instead of chess pieces. Many award-winning display designers have come up with low-cost, effective ways to set the scene for your merchandise. Here are some of them:

● Use a menu from an elegant French restaurant (or make one yourself), on a white cloth-covered table along with a champagne bottle (empty) and two crystal wine glasses to set the stage for evening clothes or quality glassware.

● Drift white sand across the floor, add a few interesting shells, that piece of driftwood, a pair of sunglasses, and a bottle of upscale suntan lotion tumbling out of a summer tote bag. Voila! You've created a beach scene for your swimsuit promotion or sunglass sale.

● Borrow a park bench (or rent it, if you must) and surround it with artificial blooming fruit boughs to create an aura of spring.

● A couple of tennis rackets, a spill of balls, and some sunglasses will make a perfect setting for active sportswear.

● If you're featuring cottons or, perhaps, wash-and-wear dresses, hang them from a clothesline with big, old-fashioned clothespins.

● A playbill, opera glasses, and an evening bag will make elegant scenery to draw attention to your theater fashions.

● A clutch of pine boughs, real or artificial, sprayed with fake snow can provide the perfect background for a display of furs or winter coats. Pile fluffy snow on the floor, too.

● A brightly colored umbrella or two and clear cellophane strips hanging from the ceiling to simulate rain will draw all eyes to your display of raincoats.

● Try posing a mannequin wearing an exquisite slip or robe in front of a full-length mirror studying her reflection with her back to the public. Most people won't be able to resist stopping to discover what the front of the garment looks like.

● Create an effect of opulence with a heap of satin-covered pillows on which you've draped fake diamond necklaces and bracelets. A good setting for sensuous black night wear or underthings.

● Travel posters, timetables, and a sprinkle of cancelled tickets (from a travel agent) plus a suitcase or two create the mood for a display of vacation fashions. They will add zip to a luggage display, too.

● Instead of showing a dress on a mannequin, fasten it with wire to heavy poster board. Add an artist's fashion sketch to establish a "designer" theme.

● A potted Easter lily or two, a handsome Bible (your family's or from a bookstore), and a few colored eggs will shout "Easter" and provide the setting for a spring display.

● A portable typewriter and a stack of books amid typing paper scattered across the floor sets the tone for back-to-school fashions, school supplies, even typewriters and small computers.

● If you've run an ad announcing "garden-fresh prints," set the display stage for them with a rake and fork, perhaps even a wheelbarrow (depending on the size of the space you have to work with). Borrow all these items from a nearby garden center and give credit on a small card in the display.

● A picnic basket with supplies tumbling out onto a red-and-white checked picnic cloth defines a mood for hot-weather leisure clothes.

Don't hesitate to ask managers of other stores in your community or mall to lend you props for unusual displays. Always give the lender credit and return borrowed items promptly. You'll find you can create any setting or mood and make more of those passersby stop long enough to be tempted into your store.

Chapter Six:
MAKE THE MOST
OF YOUR SPACE

Even if it is only a former closet or a corner you've stolen from a stock or receiving room, the layout of your office should leave no doubt that it *is* your office. Use a sturdy ceiling-to-floor pegboard partition to isolate it from the rest of the area. Hang a jumbo bulletin board on the wall above your desk, where you can survey it frequently. Situate your desk so that when you're sitting at it your back will be to employees who enter the area. Let them know that you are not to be casually interrupted any more than you would be if you were in a walled office with the door closed.

In front of you hang a large calendar with big daily spaces where you can list your appointments and other items you must remember. Post your "to do today" list there, also. When you see these memory joggers every time you sit at the desk you're less likely to overlook an important task or meeting.

Furnishings for your space should be kept to a minimum. Select a small desk, even one called a "student desk." You'll need a filing cabinet, too, preferably one with a lock.

To set up a filing system you'll need file folders, labels, and guides. Don't try to file purchase orders in one drawer, bills in another, and correspondence in still another. File them all together, alphabetically, using colors to enable you to find exactly what you want easily and quickly.

Choose a different color file folder and label for each category of information. Say you want to look up your latest order to ABC Company. Go to the "A" section of your file and look for a pink folder, since you have made pink the color for purchase orders. Paste a color-key to the front of the file cabinet so you and your people will remember what each color signifies.

Some experts recommend using different "cut" positions for the file folder tabs, as well as colored folders. You can specify whether the tab will appear at the left-hand corner of the folders, one-quarter of the way to the right, in the center, and so on. Just ask the clerk at your office supply store for assistance. Having tabs in different positions makes it possible for you to even more quickly identify and sort folders by category.

Each alphabetic section such as *A to C, D to F,* and so on, should contain file folders labeled with the names of companies or people beginning with those letters. In the section encompassing *S,* for example, you could have a pink folder labeled *Smith* and containing the purchase orders for the Smith Company. You could also have a blue folder labeled *Smith* holding invoices from the Smith Company and a yellow one for correspondence with that firm. In the folders, documents are arranged by date, with the most recent in front.

Keep a shallow basket on top of the filing cabinet. In it collect papers to be filed and try to empty it at least once each day, so you won't find yourself wasting time searching for documents. Filing becomes an onerous chore only when it's allowed to accumulate.

Keep some *OUT* cards in that file basket, too. These are single-thickness cards the size and shape of your file folders. (Such cards are sold at office supply stores, but you can easily make them by pasting together the sides of ordinary folders). Each person who removes a folder from the file must sign his or her name and the date on the out card and slip it into the space where the folder belongs. Using out cards may seem like a time-consuming chore not needed in a small business, but it protects vital documents from loss because of careless handling.

You'll want to keep the top of your desk as free of clutter as possible, but there are some things that belong there. One is a rotary address file--Rolodex, for example--where your system of colors will come in handy once again. Place strips of tape in appropriate colors at the very top of the white cards. Thus, if you need the phone number or address of vendor Smith Company, just whirl your rotary file to *S* and look for a green-stripped (signifying a vendor) card.

You may find a desk-top index card file more practical. On 3-by-5-inch cards you can record more information about vendors than you can squeeze on rotary file cards. You may also keep your customer mailing list in this file. Identify them by a strip of tape in a color you haven't used for another category. It might be helpful to sort them by zip code, as well as by the alphabet, too. An index card file is also an excellent place to store shipping information.

A bookstore owner says he keeps track of his inventory on index cards. "I make a card for every different item in my store," he says. "I enter the date of purchase and a little circle for each copy I put in stock. As I sell the books I fill in the circles with colors representing the month each unit was sold." He adds that he always knows how fast a particular item is selling and how many he has on hand. This technique might be a little clumsy for some items, but you might adapt it to accessories, jewelry, small appliances, and so on. If you put suppliers' names on the cards, reordering will be a snap.

Your tickler file can also be kept in a card file. Put tabs for all 12 months on a set of dividers and tabs for 31 days. Start with *January* in the front with the daily cards right behind. In a tickler file you place reminders of invitations you've accepted, the date on which you must pay your insurance premium, when to file tax returns, any item on which you must follow up. At month's end, move *January* to the back and put *February* in front of the daily guides.

On your pegboard partition suspend two or three shelves to create a bookcase without using any floor space. Keep often-used volumes on a shelf within easy reach of the desk and you have at your fingertips all the materials you need to keep your business running smoothly. No matter how small it is, your office can be efficient and tidy.

SECTION II:
KEEPING RECORDS

Chapter Seven:
INVENTORY

Since inventory is usually the biggest asset on your balance sheet, controlling it should be at the top of your priority list. Many store owners think taking a careful physical count once or twice a year is controlling inventory; it's not. Because inventory control is half of merchandise management--the critical aspect of your business--it must be a continuous process.

Merchandise management consists of planning and controlling inventory so as to maintain a balance between the expectations of customers and the demands of your financial strategy. Once a periodic plan is complete, control comes into play. It, too, consists of two parts: Comparing actual sales with planned sales and adjusting plans when performance fails to meet your goals. Clearly, control records--often called status sheets, since they indicate the status of the inventory--should be a primary source of information for your next round of planning.

The objectives of a good inventory control system are seven: 1) to facilitate timely reordering of merchandise, 2) to focus attention on past mistakes so they won't happen again, 3) to reveal promptly all slow-selling items so they can be marked down and moved out, 4) to show what vendor lines are most popular, 5) to evaluate promotional events with an eye to discontinuing those that aren't worth what they cost, 6) to provide necessary data for periodic revision of your basic stock list, and 7) to make selling easier because of improved assortments and fresher stocks.

Surely a little extra record keeping is a small price to pay to accomplish so many desirable ends. The method that can yield such important results for your business is perpetual unit control, continuous posting of sales and merchandise receipts, including any adjustments for customer returns and returns to vendors. With that data available, stock on hand is calculated by adding stock additions to beginning inventory and subtracting units sold. Physical counts done once or twice each year verify the accuracy of your ongoing process.

If yours is a small store with a modest inventory, you should have no problem devising a satisfactory manual system. On the other hand, if your inventory is large or you have several stores, you might want to look into a POS (point of sale) register that does much of the work for you. These sophisticated devices record sales data onto tape or disk memory that can be used as input for an inventory control computer program.

To institute a unit-control system you must first list everything you want to get from the system. Then examine the various means of collecting the desired information to determine which one is best for you. You might have your salespeople record the details of all sales on sales checks, with carbon copies going to the control office, where they will be sorted by classification and the data posted to appropriate control records.

Or you may choose to use a control ticket printed with the desired information and attached to each unit when it is placed in stock. The ticket (or a stub) is removed when the item (or package) is sold. Extreme care must be taken to replace tickets on items that are returned by customers and to show returned merchandise on control records.

Once you have decided how to collect the information you need, you'll want to devise forms necessary to do the job: the control record, one for each different style number in your inventory; the price ticket that will be placed on each garment; the sales check, or sales register receipt. Next take a complete physical inventory so you have a good starting point.

Now mark each item in your inventory with the data you want to capture: style number, size, color, vendor, retail price, and cost (in code) are probably the essential bits of data you'll need, but you may discover others you want.

Finally, devise a means of tabulating and summarizing sales. Data should be posted daily, if possible, and summarized once a week if the system is to yield all the benefits you expect.

At any moment you should be able to look at a unit control record and see that the item is moving rapidly and needs to be reordered or that it needs to be marked down for quick sale. You'll discover, perhaps, that one style dress is selling in yellow, but not in blue; that size 14s of another style are moving, but 10s are not. An effective inventory control system can put you where you belong: in charge of your merchandise.

Chapter Eight:
KEEPING RECORDS MANUALLY

Your inventory records are like a roll of exposed film. They have to be developed before you can see the complete picture. Just as most amateur photographers let someone else process their film, most retailers seek help when it comes to developing an inventory control system and organizing the reams of information such a system yields.

But in today's high-tech world it's pretty hard to find help with manual record keeping. Firms who will run your records through their computers fill several yellow pages of the phone book; firms who will sell you a small computer and set up an inventory control system are almost as numerous. It takes some digging, however, to unearth someone to help with your manual records.

Your search should start with the nearest office of the Small Business Administration. Ask for a "Request for Counseling" form, a very simple, single-sheet document on which you ask for free management assistance from the SBA. Some member of SCORE (Service Corps of Retired Executives) will be asked to try to advise you. (Record keeping assistance isn't the only kind of help you can request. They'll also attempt to help with your problems in increasing sales, advertising, market research, sources of credit and financing, and so on). This government service can only get you started, however, or recommend sources of continuing assistance.

To locate long-time help, you should next check the yellow pages of your phone book. Under headings such as *Business Forms* and *Accounting Systems*, look for companies that offer not only forms necessary for setting up inventory control systems, but also continuing advice and assistance. While most of these advertisers don't purport to do the record keeping analysis for you, they do claim to supply you with the forms to make the task simple and foolproof. Perhaps you could hire a college student to do the actual work on a part-time basis, while you devote your own time and energy to more creative tasks.

Blackbourn Systems, Inc.; 1821 University Avenue; St. Paul, MN 55104, provides a general business bookkeeping system that claims to consist of "quick, easy entries." The well-known Pegboard "one-write" system for small and medium businesses is sold by Burroughs Business Systems and Forms; P.O. Box 27;

Claymont, DE 19703. Burroughs says their systems are installed and serviced by local representatives.

Ideal System: Inventory Management System #5900 is sold for $9.95 by Dymo Visual Systems, Inc.; P.O. Box 1568; Augusta, GA 30903. This system is said to "show at a glance your inventory position by item, what to order and when, its value, prime and alternate suppliers." Safeguard Business Systems, Inc., offers a number of one-write systems designed to save time and help small business owners with record keeping. Systems are installed and serviced by local representatives. You can get a free "Business Systems Reference Manual" by writing to Safeguard at 470 Maryland Drive; Fort Washington, PA 19034.

Still another source of forms and assistance is Whitehill Systems,Division of Small Business Advisors, Inc.; 48 West 48th Street; New York, NY 10036. This group proclaims itself to be "A nationwide organization devoted to counseling small and medium sized businesses with emphasis on recordkeeping systems. . . . Local business counselors review and analyze recordkeeping requirements; furnish a complete set of records; provide personal instructions on use and maintenance of records. . . . provide guidance throughout the year." Their service includes a monthly tax bulletin with up-to-date tax information and money-saving ideas. You can phone Whitehill at (212) 869-9642.

The National Retail Merchants Association (NRMA) offers two publications designed to help owners of smaller stores learn to handle their inventory chores. The first, *Merchandise Control and Budgeting* (M44566) explains the fundamentals of merchandise control planning and budgeting. It includes formulas to maintain proper ratios between stocks and customer demand and is illustrated with all necessary forms for maintaining inventories and also shows how to figure open-to-buy. It costs NRMA members $7.25 and nonmembers $10.50.

The second NRMA book, *Retail Inventory Method Made Practical* (C14370), clearly explains the retail method of inventory and how it differs from the cost method, examining its advantages and disadvantages. The 70 pages include sample forms for recording merchandise transfers, sales, price changes, open-to-buy, and much more. Cost to NRMA members is $4.75, nonmembers $6.75. To obtain either of these books write to National Retail Merchants Association; 100 West 31st Street; New York, NY 10001.

"Retailers today," says Dan Friedman of Fashion Business Systems, "cannot change the cost of their rent, their advertising, their payroll. The only thing they can change is the cost of goods." Friedman says if you can buy more efficiently and take advantage of having the right merchandise in your store at the right time, that's how you'll make money. Since his firm sells computerized inventory systems, his remarks are aimed at specialty store owners who are in the market for small business computers and systems. Friedman's opinion, however, is echoed by L. H. Joseph, Jr., an inventory management consultant of Los Angeles, who adds, "If you haven't got a sound manual concept, you haven't got a system that can be computerized." Joseph's firm is an international organization whose members travel all over the country to assist retailers. He admits, however, that--since he charges for travel time and all expenses--the cost of his services would probably be prohibitive for most small retailers.

It appears that business forms suppliers and the Small Business Administration are your best hope of getting help with your inventory control problems. Be sure to examine thoroughly any system you consider installing to be sure it will do the job for your particular needs, that it won't be too complex and time consuming to be helpful, and that it is designed so you can easily convert to a computer when the size of your business warrants that expense.

Chapter Nine:
CONTROLLING INVENTORY

An item in the financial news reported that one of the largest department store operators in the nation had posted record revenue and earnings for a recent quarter. The company was said to have attributed the earnings increase in large part to lower markdowns and better inventory management. The message underlying that news item is clear: To maximize profits you must exercise good control over your inventory.

Maintaining effective control over stock can be critical to a small retail operation. At the very least, an unbalanced stock can lead to lost sales and unhappy customers or debilitating markdowns on slow-moving merchandise. Your system doesn't need to be elaborate, but it should tell you what you need to order by showing what is on hand, what is on order, and what has been sold. Analysis of this information can help you meet customer demand, pinpoint trends, evaluate merchandise performance. And all that can be accomplished with a manual system of recordkeeping.

The kinds and number of records a retail store manager needs will depend on the number of items in the store and the depth of detail desired. Stock control may be accomplished by counting stock or sales. In either case, a model stock list is the starting point.

A model stock list is simply a list of all items involving styles, colors, and sizes. It should include "model stock" quantities, the amounts needed to maintain an "in stock" position for a given period--usually a number of weeks. The period of time to be covered can be calculated by a simple formula: reorder period + delivery period = number of weeks.

Suppose that you order blouses every six weeks and delivery from the vendor takes two weeks. Your number of weeks to be covered by the model quantity would be eight. If you sell an average of ten of these blouses each week, you would need 80 (10 x 8) to maintain your stock. When size is a factor, as with the blouses, your knowledge of your customers will tell you how many of each size should make up the 80 units.

The model stock list for an apparel store should include a special section, called maintained selection items, flagging groups of items that change with tastes in fashion, items that can be substituted for each other. Dresses are an obvious example. When your current stock of seasonal dresses reaches the reorder point, you will probably want to replace them with a new style. Merchandise of this type should be listed on reorder records in groups by classification, item, and price. Such a listing will insure stocking a given price line at all times with proper merchandise. At the same time, it provides a record of the sales activity on individual styles.

All effective inventory control begins with counting. You can count stock on a periodic basis or you can count it daily by counting sales. The best method for you depends on the number of items involved and on which one will give the most up-to-date information at the least cost.

If you count stock, you'll need to have for each item a tally card listing how many units are on hand, how many have been ordered, how many have been received, and how many have been sold. About every two weeks you'll count your stock to verify the cards and analyze sales. You then decide whether to close out an item, order fill-ins, or increase the order quantity, if an item is moving more rapidly than anticipated.

Perhaps your merchandise mix can be more effectively controlled by counting sales. If you use this method, you keep track of sales when they are made, item by item. Price tickets should be attached to garments on arrival and should indicate style, color, size, vendor, and the like. Unless you have a sophisticated cash register that will show this data on the register tape, you'll want to use a price ticket with a stub that can be removed for record keeping. Daily tabulation of stubs will provide data about which items are selling best, which colors, sizes, and styles are the most popular. Without ticket stubs, sales personnel will need to write sales slips that include all pertinent information about every item sold.

Whether information comes from register tapes, sales slips, or price tickets, it has to be analyzed frequently. The best way is to summarize the data and post it daily to inventory ledger sheets. These stock records provide the information you need to order fill-ins, calculate turnover, and so on.

One goal of an inventory control system is to assure that an excessive amount of working capital isn't tied up in merchandise. Another goal is the maintenance of a balanced assortment of merchandise to meet customers' needs. Open-to-buy is the key to keeping stocks in line. Open-to-buy is the amount of merchandise (in units or dollars) you need to receive into stock during a given period. The period may be the selling season that is customary for a certain line of merchandise or a time span set by the store manager. At the start of the period, a merchandise class-ification--such as blouses--is open to receive the number of units necessary to achieve the sales you anticipate for the period. Suppose, for example, you expect to sell 200 blouses. To start the season you buy and receive 160; you are open to buy an additional 40 blouses. The 40 is your control figure when you order fill-in stock. As long as you buy no more than 40 during the period, your investment in blouses will be no greater than you had planned.

But what happens if customers make a run on the blouses? If sales are exceptionally good early in the season and you can get a new stock within the next several weeks, the question is a merchandising one. If your good judgment tells you the upturn in blouse sales is a lasting trend, you increase your open-to-buy for the item.

An inventory control system is essential to your store's prosperity. No system, however, can be a substitute for your experience and judgment. What you get out of your system will depend on your collecting the right information and asking the right questions when you analyze results.

Chapter Ten:
STOCKTURN--YARDSTICK
OF SUCCESS

Are you always out of something or--worse yet--never out of anything? If so, it's probably because your inventory is out of balance. One way to measure the degree of balance of your inventory is to calculate its turnover rate, how quickly goods move through your store. Turnover, a financial ratio commonly calculated for a year, is the number of times the average inventory has been sold and replaced during a given period. It is arrived at by dividing the retail dollar value of net sales for the period under consideration by the average inventory at selling price. If your store's turnover rate is too low it may be that your prices are too high or that your stock is poorly planned in relation to your customers' buying habits.

Everything else being equal, the higher the turnover the better. You must take care, however, that in seeking a high turnover rate you don't end up with excessive stockouts, always a dangerous situation. On the other hand, buying in large quantities to avoid running out can result in too many markdowns of merchandise that has lingered too long on the sales floor. In the average women's store, about 80 percent of the sales comes from merchandise fewer than 90 days old. Thus, slow stockturn can decrease your sales.

Limiting the amount of money you have tied up in inventory at any one time reduces such expenses as interest, insurance, taxes. It also reduces the amount of space you need to store goods. Turnover that is too rapid, however, can lead to what is called a "hand-to-mouth" buying policy. Such a policy increases clerical costs in writing frequent purchase orders, higher shipping rates, and loss of quantity discounts. Some retailers practice hand-to-mouth buying when designers and trade publications predict a major change in women's styles, but general acceptance by consumers is iffy. A wholehearted believer in rapid turnover is Jim Dixon of Retail Merchandising Service Automation (RMSA) in Riverside, California. "The faster you can turn the inventory," he says, "the more you minimize the investment up front while increasing profits."

Dixon says it's impossible to predict what any store's turnover rate should be, or even to calculate a meaningful average for stores of the same type. "We don't subscribe to the concept that there's any kind of an average that's terribly meaningful. Average turnover is just that," he insists. "It's going to be a roll-up of all the different kinds of turns available." He adds, "The programs that we have developed are geared to optimize turn within a given classification of merchandise, like--say--dresses, or whatever, for each individual store." He points out that a retailer with 100 different stores might have 100 different turnover goals customized for each store. "Whatever the store is capable of doing is the rate at which it should be operating."

One of the critical aspects of turnover, according to Dixon, is separating merchandise into classifications. He points out that a retailer cannot calculate turnover for lingerie and suits as a single ratio. You probably won't need to separate bras and slips when working out the turnover rate, however. And, Dixon points out, a lower turnover rate is acceptable for staple items such as lingerie and most accessories. You will, however, need to consider the turnover of $40 dresses as separate from that of $100 dresses, because they'll have different sales patterns. "You'll find," he says, "as you go into higher-priced goods, the sales patterns definitely change. Look at cocktail dresses going for more than $1,000 and you'll find that people who buy that type of commodity are buying it very, very close to when they want it, which is early in season." He goes on, "When you get into middle-America merchandise, retailers typically supply the goods and consumers buy them toward the middle or end of the season."

Classification merchandising is the secret, according to Dixon, of using stock turnover figures to your advantage. It's just as bad to be missing business because you're underinventoried as it is to have too much inventory. Typically, however, being underinventoried is not usually a problem with a specialty store. Classifications that are really moving tend to be underinventoried while two or three classes will be moving more slowly and, hence, overinventoried. It's a matter of pinpointing where you stand by classification and then coming up with actions to rectify the problem and prevent it from happening again. Dixon says his firm designs systems that show you how much inventory you need to minimize your investment to get the necessary return on it.

The Small Business Administration booklet on inventory control for small business (Small Business Management Series number 41, about $4.50) says, "One of the best ways to measure how well you are managing inventory is to determine the activity of stock in relation to your volume of business. This can be computed from your balance sheet and profit-and-loss statement using an inventory turnover formula such as: Total annual sales volume divided by average inventory valuation equals inventory turnover." For example, if your annual sales figure for one class of merchandise is $70,000 and average inventory of that item is $10,000, turnover rate is seven times a year. The turnover rate tells you if your purchasing and inventory policies are sound.

Turnover rate comparisons should be made between your company's present and past performances and the ratios of businesses similar to yours. You must always bear in mind, however, that each store is unique. Just because your store has a turnover figure equal to the national average doesn't mean that it's operating at the best level. Conditions may be such that too many sales are being lost because of a lack of merchandise breadth.

Because inventories represent such a significant portion of your store's assets, you should keep close tabs on them. Annual turnover should be recalculated monthly. Each month you should add that month's sales figures and subtract the sales for the thirteenth month prior, and then recalculate the average inventory for the new 12-month period. Keeping these figures up to date for all major classifications of merchandise is like keeping your finger on the pulse of your business. You'll always know if it's thriving or starting to have problems.

To insure rapid turnover in any season, according to RMSA, you must strive to order all merchandise so that it arrives approximately 30 days prior to the seasonal debut. Then it is crucial that you advertise and display your new arrivals. Since customers rarely plan their purchases in advance, only adequate promotion can attract the impulse buyer. As the season progresses, keep an eye out for hot-selling items that you can reorder. Proper timing of deliveries, promotion, and reorders is the key to maintaining a high turnover rate without losing sales because of stockouts.

Once you have succeeded in raising the level of turnover in every classification, you will be well on the way to reaching retailing success. Your merchandise will be fresh and exciting at all times and you will be taking fewer markdowns while seeing both volume of sales and profits go up.

SECTION III:
PROMOTIONS

Chapter Eleven:
WHY LOSS LEADERS?

Loss leaders are a promotional device that almost all retailers use at least once in a while. Leaders are, of course, pieces of merchandise you advertise at low markups in order to attract customers to your store. The idea, obviously, is that when customers come to buy advertised leaders, they will buy other items at regular prices. The term *loss leader* is applied to an item priced at less than your total cost, including shipping and overhead.

Several states have unfair-sales laws, unfair-trade acts, or sales-below-cost laws that seek to protect retailers from competitors who might sell leader items at considerably less than cost. Large discount merchandisers are sometimes willing to absorb substantial losses in order to drive competitors from the field. Laws banning such tactics are designed to protect small retailers from unfair competition.

Maine's Unfair Sales Act, fairly typical of the general statutes, requires retailers to charge a margin of at least 5.75 percent above invoice cost for all goods except damaged or deteriorated items. Lower prices may be charged, however, if the retailer can demonstrate beyond a doubt that the cost of doing business is less than 5.75 percent. Arizona's law requires a markup of at least 12 percent and California's forbids sales below cost except to meet competition. Cost, however, is defined as invoice or replacement cost, whichever is lower, plus the dealer's cost of doing business. Very few of these laws have been enforced aggressively and many states are examining their retailing laws and repealing those that have proved too difficult to enforce or too unpopular with consumers.

Laws or no laws, loss leaders are a popular policy, motivated by the need to stimulate store traffic, particularly in a time of sagging sales. Getting a customer into the store, however, is only the first round in the merchandising battle. If she walks in, looks at the leader item--perhaps even buying it--and walks out again without spending a dollar on regular-priced items, the tactic has failed, unless her perception of your store is so positive that she will return another time to buy full-priced merchandise.

Clearly, the use of loss leaders involves more than just lowering the price on an item or two. Prices of merchandise other than the leaders must be set carefully. Specials will attract bargain hunters who may be disenchanted with your store if they suspect nonadvertised items have been raised too much. Moreover, overlarge reductions are likely to repel shoppers, rather than attract them. If the price of a leader is so low that customers suspect it must be inferior merchandise, perhaps even seconds, your store's image will suffer.

Ideally the loss leader is a brand name item that is fairly inexpensive and appeals to a great number of people. It must particularly appeal to impulse buyers, women who are window shopping in your mall or neighborhood and see a window banner announcing the leader. Finally, the perfect loss leader is an item that customers buy in quantity or replace fairly often. Pantyhose come immediately to mind. Most women are constantly on the lookout for pantyhose that are sheer, comfortable, and low priced.

Expensive items, no matter how deeply reduced, do not make good leaders. In the first place, few women are shopping for, say, fur stoles at any given moment, and few furs are bought on impulse. Finally, once a woman has bought something as expensive as a fur, she has probably exhausted the amount of money she is--at least psychologically--ready to spend at the time. Thus, no matter what her economic status, she probably won't be interested in any regular-priced merchandise.

Exercise shorts might make good leaders; so could panties, scarves, sweaters, plain blouses, even half-slips. Such apparel items will work especially well as leaders if they have a label shoppers recognize and identify as being good quality, usually higher priced.

If buying the leader inspires most customers to buy a related item, the promotion will be truly successful. If your promotional item is panties, for example, you might want to have matching or coordinated bras and half slips displayed in the same area. Or perhaps you made a good buy on plaid skirts. Use them as featured leaders and display--or advertise--right next to the skirts' matching jackets at full price.

The loss leader you choose to promote will determine what type of customers will respond to your ads. Ideally, those customers will be ones who will shop your store regularly long after the promotion is ended. You don't want to attract women who normally buy their clothing at K-Mart and won't even enter your store until you next advertise a bargain price they recognize.

Another important aspect of deciding what merchandise to feature is freshness. Your leaders must be current, timely items. Bathing suits in November or prom dresses in August will be perceived as clearance items, not leaders. If, on the other hand, you could buy enough beach tote bags to promote them at low, low prices in late June, you could probably show them alongside swimsuits and cover-ups and do a landslide business.

Be sure you select popular items, too, for your leaders. Dresses that haven't moved off the rack since you received them aren't good choices for leaders. Touting stale merchandise to new customers could damage your reputation for being up to the minute with new fashions. Advertise slow movers as close-out or clearance items. If you could, however, manage to buy a good selection of stylish summery cottons in time to feature them in August's waning days of summer, you'd no doubt have a winning loss leader that would entice new customers into your store just when you're starting to show back-to-school merchandise.

Be sure that you have an adequate supply of whatever you promote as a leader or state prominently in your ads that "quantities are severely limited." You don't want to antagonize customers by seeming to use bait-and-switch tactics, advertising low prices to get customers in the door and then trying to divert them away from the leaders in favor of more expensive items.

Like all advertising and most promotions, loss leaders can do no more than get customers through your front door. What those shoppers do after they enter the store is what makes any promotion succeed or fail. Your salespeople must be prepared to deal pleasantly with a possible invasion of bargain hunters. They must have sales goals and stick to them. But most importantly, the only way loss leaders can truly stimulate business is if most customers who come in to buy the leader buy at least one other regular-priced item. That's where your sales staff shows its mettle.

Everyone on the sales floor must remember to go further than just asking, "Will there be anything else?" Have a game plan for added sales worked out in advance. If your leader is the tote bags, for example, salespeople might suggest, "This swimsuit and cover-up would be great for your vacation, too." Or, in the case of the reduced-price skirts, the sales staff should suggest not only the matching jackets, but also blouses and scarves to make a complete outfit. Loss leaders that are aggressively followed up in that manner can be a valuable promotional tool.

Chapter Twelve:
HOLIDAY EVENTS

The holiday selling season is almost upon you once again and you're probably wondering what on earth you can do this year that isn't just a rerun of promotions you've tried in the past. Or perhaps you remember the "Men's Night Out" you staged last year; almost nobody came. How can you make sure all this year's promotions are successful?

You'll want to be creative, different. Don't put on a promotion just because another store in the mall or down the street has done it. And don't undertake one simply because it's what you've always done. In fact, this might be the year to promise yourself you'll do something different all season long.

To accomplish these ends, and a lot more, put the postal service to work for you. Plan an intensive campaign that addresses shoppers who've already shown interest in your store: those whose names are on your mailing list. But before you drop a single envelope into a mailbox, have a talk with someone at your post office. Ask how special mailing rates can save you money while boosting holiday sales. If you'll be sending out at least 500 first-class pieces or 200 bulk-mail flyers or catalogs in a single mailing, you might be wise to buy permits to use "presorted first class mail" and "bulk mailing." Each will cost $50, but will no doubt pay for themselves in two or three mailings. You don't have to buy a postage meter or any fancy equipment; you just fill out some relatively simple forms and pay the fee. Someone at the post office will give you instructions on how to sort, stamp, and deposit your mail. Costs will vary widely, depending on how many pieces you're sending out, what class of mail you use, and the contents of the pieces. However, you could save as much as five cents on each item you mail.

Christmas Club. So what are you going to mail? You might want to launch a club plan first. Why should Christmas Clubs be limited to banks? Send flyers to everyone on your mailing list inviting them to join by signing up the next time they visit your store. There's no application fee, of course. From now until Christmas Eve, Club members will save register tapes or receipts from every purchase. By totaling the value of purchases made during the Club period they can select–without additional cost–anything selling for a certain amount. Say $200 in register tapes will get them an item priced at $10.

Make the Club even more exciting by assigning added value to certain purchases. Perhaps you're going to push a particular line of sleepwear one week.

During that period, each tape from a sale of the specified line will be counted as double its face value at redemption time. The bonus items can be a special group of slips or bras, anything you want to move fast. You might even want to specify a different bonus item every week for the duration of the promotion. The more ways you find to keep the Christmas Club exciting, the more it will increase your season's business.

Ornament Offer. If you're looking for a way to increase foot traffic in your store while adding to your mailing list, announce in your newspaper ads that you will give, free, a special Christmas ornament to anyone who comes in and fills out a blank that includes all her mail and phone information and answers a couple of questions about sizes, preferred lines, whatever you'd like to know about potential customers. You should be able to buy a large quantity of attractive ornaments from a wholesaler for a price that won't make the promotion too expensive. Run this promotion early in the season so you will have an expanded mailing list to use during the balance of the holiday shopping period.

Coupon Book. Send flyers to all your customers announcing a Holiday Coupon Book Program. Everyone who spends at least $100 (or any amount you choose) during a single visit between December 1 and 24 will receive a book of discount coupons redeemable during specified weeks all next year. The coupons can be for certain items, say slips from a particular lingerie maker, or panties by one of your good suppliers. Or, if you prefer, coupons can be applied to any purchases made during each period. Boost holiday sales and increase store traffic throughout the coming year.

A variation on the coupon book promotion could be to mail one to every customer early in the holiday shopping season. Let each coupon represent a specified discount--dollar or percentage--on a particular item or class. A brand of hosiery, say, or any dreamy nightgown. If the coupons are for holiday wear or garments especially appropriate for gifts, the promotion will seem more seasonal.

Grant a Wish. A promotion that is especially appealing is "Tag Your Dream." You send to every woman on your mailing list a letter explaining how the promotion works and enclosing a two-part tag. (Make it in holiday colors or in some traditional holiday shape.) Give each recipient a week or so--certainly no more than two weeks--to bring the tag in and attach it to the one item in your store she would like to get for Christmas. Only one tag is permitted per item, so it will pay your customers to respond quickly to tag the negligee sets, mixers, whatever they dream of owning. Stubs from the tags go in a box near the cash register. At the end of the promotion you draw the winning stub and award the item to the customer whose name and address are on the matching tag.

Holiday Greetings. A very simple promotion but one that's sure to build good will is a greeting card. Send each of your customers a card or note thanking her for her patronage and including a coupon for a small discount on a purchase she makes during the holiday season. Or ask her to pick up her gift--perhaps a small poinsettia plant--the next time she's in your store, while supplies last, of course. This device makes certain that more of your regular customers will visit your store during the season. If possible, address these greetings by hand and send them by first-class mail so they'll look like part of your customers' regular holiday mail.

Fifty Nifty Gift Ideas. How about mailing out a catalog of, say, *Fifty Nifty Gift Ideas* for the whole family? This is a catalog of gifts for all members of the family to give the women on their lists. A full-color booklet will be the most appealing, if you can afford it. Include gifts in all price ranges and merchandise classes. You may want to use the "Gifts under $10 and Gifts under $25" approach, or divide the booklet into shopping hints for men, women, and children. Kids who are looking for nice gifts for their moms are good prospects for a promotion of this type. Petticoats, hosiery, camisoles might fall within kids' budgets. Alluring lingerie, robes, special sexy garter belts are good ideas for the men's section.

Men's Night Out. You can use a variation on the catalog promotion and tie it to your Men's Night Party. Include in the catalog a "Wish List" blank on which your customer can list the items she hopes to receive. Ask her to include her sizes and the names and addresses of the men she expects to be shopping for her gifts. Offer her a small discount or special gift for bringing the list to the store by a specified date.

You then send hand-addressed invitations to a "Stag Party" fashion show to all those men. Word the invitation to let the men know that you have the wish lists and size information to help them choose from the selection they'll see on attractive models during the evening. Schedule the party for an evening fairly late in the season: Men don't get into the Christmas shopping mood as early as women do. And tell them you'll have assistants--perhaps the models--to make the shopping still more fun. Be sure to specify that admission will be by invitation only, but you might want to announce in your ads that shoppers not on the mailing list can pick up catalogs at your store. Be sure that anyone who does ask for a catalog gives you data for future mailings.

A Lucky Twist. An added twist for this promotion is the "lucky cup." Reveal in the invitation that cups or glasses for the champagne--or Perrier, or whatever you serve--will be numbered for an exciting drawing. One lucky shopper will be refunded the price of all the purchases he makes during the party. Near the end of the event you draw the lucky number and the man whose glass bears that number gets free everything he bought during the evening. This device is almost guaranteed to insure a good response to your invitations. And it may stimulate even tight-fisted shoppers to be a little less cautious as they select gifts.

Prize-Winning Message. Print a special message on some, but not all, of a batch of direct mail flyers. Instruct the recipients of the flyers to bring them to the store to learn what they've won. Everyone with a special message gets at least a small discount; some winners receive nice prizes from your stock or gifts you've purchased. If you're running a newspaper ad about the same time, include the notice, "Watch for your lucky flyer. It may entitle you to a very special gift." Customers will read the flyers carefully, looking for the message, and not toss them out unread, if they've been alerted that there's a prize in the offing. When they come to claim their prizes, you have an opportunity to make extra sales.

A Gala Event. You might want to sponsor a "Holiday Party-Time" event at which you have demonstrations of preparing foods and beverages for seasonal parties and informal modeling of at-home and sleepwear. Enlist the aid of a delicatessen or caterer in your town to offer food tips; a beverage store owner should be able to line up someone to talk about mixed drinks or wines for the show. And you put your most enchanting holiday fashions on display. Admission is by invitation only. If you ask the businesses sharing the party with you to invite their clients, you should have a good turnout and a successful promotion.

It's easy to see from these ideas that there is no limit to the number of promotions possible and the ways to vary even the simplest theme. Let your imagination run free as you plan your holiday promotions. Then let letter carriers be the bearers of your good tidings. You'll discover it's a wonderful way to put sparkle in your holiday business.

Chapter Thirteen:
PLAYING GAMES

Everyone loves to get something free. And that's what contests and games are all about: getting something for nothing. If they are not overused and are designed to be compatible with your store image, games and contests can be an effective way to increase your store traffic and profits.

A few simple guidelines will help you devise contests that are both cost-effective and fun. When you plan any game ask yourself, *Is it too complicated? Does the sales force understand it? Does it fit my store's image?* As a general rule, choose contests based on luck, rather than skill. Judging can become too complicated and time-consuming when the test is one of skill. And be sure to publicize the names of winners so all players will consider the contest fair. When staged within these limitations, games and contests generate foot traffic, build community good will, and add names to your mailing lists. Brainstorm with your staff and friends to see how many unusual traffic building promotional events you can come up with.

Here are several ideas to get you off to a good start:

Fishing Pond. Can be a good-will event to raise money for charity, or a sales builder. Every customer gets one chance to fish for each multiple of $5.00 or $10.00 spent. Metallic fish "swimming" in a bowl are caught by a magnetic fishhook and are marked with an amount to be donated to a specified charity or a discount amount for purchases made during the shoppers' next visits to the store. Charitable donations and size of discounts are defined by how much you want to spend.

Children's Art Contest. Prizes are offered for best art work created by children from specified schools or organizations, or by children at large. Submissions are accepted at the store and are displayed for at least a week to allow plenty of proud relatives to view the exhibit. Customers get to vote for their choices by filling out ballots that include names and addresses. Prizes should be cash amounts appropriate for children.

Photography Contest. Photographs, which must include the front of your store, can be of children, pets, or family members, and must be taken on certain days and during daylight hours to eliminate lighting problems. Entries must be received within a week or so of the last shutter-snapping day. Offer prizes for the best, worst, most unusual pictures, and let the shopping public judge, again on forms that include names and addresses.

Miss [School in Your Town] Contest. Photos of contestants can be submitted by friends or family members. Winners are chosen by votes of shoppers and prizes can vary from a complete outfit to a nice sweater or jacket. All ballots must include names and addresses.

Hobby Show and Contest. Invite members of groups such as sororities, clubs, church groups, or school classes to enter craft items they've made as hobbies. Display all entries for a week or ten days before judging. Prizes are awarded for the best display, most unusual hobby, whatever you decide. A group of local dignitaries could serve as judges, or you could ask your staff to do the judging, or let shoppers vote.

Lucky Money. Make a list of the serial numbers on a quantity of one-dollar bills (how many is up to you, depending on how much you want to spend on this game). Then get the bills into general circulation in your trading area by spending them at a supermarket or other high-volume store. Each dollar is worth $5.00 or more (again depending on how much you want to spend) in purchases during a specified period.

Window Bingo. Distribute playing forms to all store visitors, then each day place one number in some out-of-the-way place in your window display or store. As with regular bingo, the first person to correctly mark off a straight line on her form is the winner. If each playing form is numbered, you can create additional winners--and more foot traffic--by posting in the store a list of lucky numbers. Add to your mailing list by conducting a drawing from nonwinning forms deposited in a box in the store.

Mystery Person. You announce in flyers, handbills, and newspaper advertising that a mystery person is abroad--in your shopping center, mall, or neighborhood. The first shopper to greet that mysterious individual with the name of your store will win a prize, which could be a substantial discount on any purchase or cash. The mystery person should be identified by a small lapel pin or a shopping bag displaying your logo, any subtle means. He or she can be in the area for as many or as few days as you choose.

Most of these games and contests require fairly modest outlays of time and money. All can be varied to suit your taste and needs and can be advertised in your regular newspaper or radio ads as well as in special mailers or handbills.

In addition, games that involve most of the community stir up a great deal of excitement and, if you submit press releases to local papers, you're likely to receive at least some free publicity. You'll discover that contests and games can be winners for your business, as well as for your customers.

Chapter Fourteen:
USING CONSULTANTS

Why would you want to put on a promotion that will help your customers spend less on clothing? To win their confidence, of course, to reinforce the image of your store as a place to achieve a look, not just to buy a dress. One way to build a strong bond between your store and your regular customers is to show them how to use accessories to update outfits they already have in their closets.

Sara McKinley Ott, a Glendale, California, fashion consultant says, "Show your customers how they can revamp outfits they have by using exciting accessories." In other words, help them achieve a new look without spending a fortune. One of the best ways to accomplish this end, according to Ott, is to announce in your ads that Ms. So-and-So, a fashion consultant (also sometimes called color consultant or image consultant) will be in your store on such and such a date. She will give a brief presentation on accessories, your ad notes, then do individual consultations. Women who want to cash in on this service can make appointments to spend some time in private consultation with the expert.

The important part of this promotion, Ott says, is to advise each woman who books an appointment to bring--or wear--an outfit she loves but wants to update for the new season or a new image. The advisor will then select from your stock accessories that are suitable to the individual and to the outfit. Belts, scarves, vests, jewelry, even sunglasses can be used to make a shopper's wardrobe look new without a huge cash outlay.

The presentation should last only about 20 minutes, Ott says, and then the consultant stays on the floor as long as need be to meet with women who have made appointments. Or, if you prefer, you may plan to have the fashion advisor available for an entire day or several hours and let shoppers queue up for advice.

In either case, you might want to serve wine and sandwiches--or other simple refreshments--to keep shoppers occupied while they wait their turn to talk to the consultant. Give the event a party atmosphere for best results. Alert your salespeople to be ready to sell suits and dresses that customers can then accessorize according to the recommendations of the consultant.

You may want to provide this service entirely free, or levy a small charge for the consultation and then deduct that amount from the cost of accessories purchased.

You might want to consider having a trunk show of individual accessories.

There are sure to be local artisans in your area who would leap at a chance to display their wares in return for a mention in your ads. It might be a small trunk full of handcrafted jewelry, say, and you have on hand a fashion expert to show how those pieces can be used to update existing wardrobes or to put finishing touches to new outfits bought during the show. Or find a scarf manufacturer who will provide a good selection for your trunk show. The fashion consultant then demonstrates all the ways scarves can be used with a single outfit to achieve many different looks.

Ott, who offers consultations to customers of Bullock's and other upscale stores in Southern California, says she charges $100 per hour for her services. She's sure, however, that in smaller communities you'll be able to find someone for a much smaller fee. "Some consultants might work for a percentage of sales," she suggests, "or even just for the publicity and referrals that will result from the presentation."

Bobby Jean Thompson of Image Reflections in Charlottesville, Virginia, has devised a "face imager" that determines the shape of a shopper's face. Using the imager, a woman can see how different scarves, necklaces, hats, and so on will look on her. Thompson, too, puts on workshops and demonstrations, charging an hourly fee for demonstrations, a flat fee for workshops. But she agrees that consultants who are just starting to build a clientele will no doubt spend a day at your store for a percentage of sales or a very small fee.

You can find the names of experts who will put on these events for you listed in the Yellow Pages under the headings "Fashion Consultants," "Image Consultants," or--sometimes--"Color Consultants." Or you can write to the Association of Fashion and Image Consultants; 7655 Old Springhouse Road; McLean, VA 22101. Brenda York, who is president of that organization, will send you a list of member consultants in your area.

Get in touch with representatives of your accessory suppliers. Ask them to recommend people who can show your customers how to use belts, beads, scarves to give their wardrobes a lift.

It will pay you to check out the credentials of any consultant you are thinking of asking to do a promotion in your store. You want to be sure the expert will give your customers honest advice without alienating them by, for example, telling them their clothes are tacky or their figures dumpy.

Showing your customers how to make the most of their wardrobes through accessorizing is a sure-fire way to win their approval and loyalty.

Chapter Fifteen:
TRUNK SHOWS--
HOWS AND WHYS

"Trunk shows are a lot of work," says Kevan Hall, head designer of Kevan Hall Unlimited, California fashion designers. "That's why we do only about 12 each year. But I enjoy doing them because I enjoy meeting the ladies and because I get so much out of the shows." Hall, who has been designing women's apparel for ten years and is a graduate of the prestigious Fashion Institute of Design in Los Angeles, creates a collection of dressy cocktail dresses and some separates. "Our clothes go from day into evening," he says, "but they're always special and dressy."

The retailers for whom Hall puts on trunk shows are usually ones with whom he has already established a relationship, stores with whom he has dealt in the past. "We have to know that the store's clients like our type of clothing," he explains, "and that they'll spend in our price bracket."

"We ask for a dollar commitment," he points out, "an order for a certain number of garments." And if the site of the trunk show isn't Los Angeles, the sponsoring retailer also pays for accommodations and travel expenses for the designer or sales representative who accompanies the fashions.

"Once an agreement has been reached on financial details," according to Hall, "we schedule the date for the show, usually a couple of months or more in advance." He says they try to pick a time when the host store's best customers will be in the city and have the money to shop for clothing. "We want to know their clients won't be traveling or trying to get their kids into school at that time," he says.

"We also expect the retailer to run an ad in the local newspaper," Hall goes on, "and to mail announcements of the show to clients." That's about all the formal preparation Hall requires, but, he notes, arrangements can be just as splashy as the retailer likes. "Wine and cheese, that sort of thing, is up to the store owner," he says, adding it can be a big event with informal modeling, or the clothes can be shown on racks around the store.

Saying that a show usually lasts two consecutive days, or on rare occasions, three, Hall points out, "We always stage them on weekdays, so the regular customers won't have to compete with weekend shoppers." A trunk show offers a woman a rare chance to receive personal attention and advice from a designer or his representative and the loyal customer shouldn't have to compete for that attention with casual shoppers.

"We spend time working with each client," says Hall, "on fitting, colors, and so on." After a client has looked at all the garments from the trunk (examples of all the designs for a particular season--perhaps 40 garments), Hall will advise her about what styles and colors will look best on her and best serve her needs, depending on her figure and lifestyle. If a garment fits and the client likes it, she can buy it on the spot, Hall explains. "Often, though," he adds, "we'll just have representative copies of garments that aren't in full production yet. Then she can order it in the size and color she wants."

"We learn a great deal at trunk shows," Hall says. These events give him information about who his clients are, how their lives are changing, what types of affairs they'll be attending in the coming seasons. "Occasionally a celebrity will drop in at a trunk show and we seize the opportunity to show our designs to that well-known person. Also, such shows give us the chance to meet the salespeople who will be handling our garments long after the show. If the salespeople are pleased with us and our designs, they'll do a better job of selling them in the future " He adds, "Sometimes the input we gather influences the designs for our next season. And, of course, the exposure doesn't hurt, either," he admits.

Hall says he thinks the sponsoring retailer stands to gain at least as much as he does. "Trunk shows, of course, generate sales," he points out. Beyond that, he notes that the store owner, too, learns more about who his or her customers are and how their lives are changing. The retailer also builds good relationships with customers through trunk shows.

A savvy retailer will discover that a classy trunk show can help define a store's customers, reinforce their loyalty, and polish the store's image, all in one fell swoop. That's getting a good return on a fairly modest investment.

Chapter Sixteen:
PUTTING ON
THE RIGHT SALE

What is a sale? Is it a short-term fix for a cash-flow problem? Is it a way to get rid of stock that didn't move the way you hoped it would? Is it a way to improve your share of the market? Is it one way you can improve your store's bottom line?

A properly planned and staged sale can be any one of those things, or several of them, as well as a means of lending excitement to your store. The key phrase, however, is "properly planned." That is, every sales promotion you put on should be held at the right time and should feature the right merchandise.

Be aware, however, that the right sale doesn't have to feature cut-price merchandise. According to a recent article in *Marketing*, "With retailers' margins continually under pressure, price cutting is not always a viable means of attracting customers. . . ." And cut-price promotions on high fashion products can damage a store's image. As a result, more fashion retailers are now putting greater emphasis on traditional sales promotion techniques in order to add value to their merchandise--and to gain an edge over their rivals.

Traditionally, women's moderate-priced, middle-America apparel stores hold clearance sales in January and July, with regular-price sales promotions in April and October. More upscale stores might add cruise/transitional clothing at the beginning of fall. And stores that appeal to college and even high school students might want to do a back-to-school promotion.

How can you tell when is the best time for *you* to hold a sale? It isn't easy. You'll want to know when the people in your immediate trading area traditionally shop for the types of merchandise you plan to feature. You'll also want to look at your sales figures for previous years to see when your customers are in the mood to buy. Finally, you will need to know if business conditions in your area make it necessary for you to adjust any of the information you've acquired. Did a recent layoff, for example, affect many of your customers? If so, they might be reluctant to spend money on expensive dresses, but eager to buy off-price merchandise.

Spend a couple of hours each week at the library, reading the likes of *The Wall Street Journal, Business Week*, and *Women's Wear Daily* to stay abreast of national business trends. Study the business sections of local newspapers and pay close attention to financial items on TV and radio for changes in the local scene.

Use that information to adjust seasonal sales patterns you are familiar with.

Says Richard Widney, vice president of marketing for the Retail Merchandising Service Automation (RMSA), adviser to thousands of retailers across the land, "We look at sales from the viewpoint of industry practice." He says the theory is that if most of your competitors are having a sale, you should be having one also.

"In the fashion industry," Widney points out, "the best reason for having sales is changing seasons, with the attendant need to move out merchandise left over from the previous season." He adds, "We aren't in favor of [price reduction] sales, per se. If you know something isn't selling well as you're going through the season, you ought to take a small markdown on it right away rather than have to take a big markdown at season's end." He says the most successful of RMSA's clients do that.

Widney and other retailing experts insist that repeated reduced-price sales get consumers into the mode of always waiting for sales to shop. Then shoppers reason, "There will always be a sale somewhere. All I have to do is watch the paper and if it isn't my favorite store [holding a sale], it'll be some other store." From that standpoint, Widney says, sales are bad. "We encourage shops to have various kinds of sales events." They should be promotional, not just price reductions. It might be a swimsuit sale in July, for some shops, but maybe it's a Mother's day promotion or something early in the holiday season. Perhaps you'll do a little direct mail ahead of time to coax men to come in for help with their gift shopping. That's the kind of sale that stirs up excitement and doesn't require markdowns. "Anybody can lower prices and give away all their profits," says Widney. "The trick is to keep a good balance."

You're sure to see an improvement in profits if you plan seasonal promotions, not constant off-price sales. Such sales can add excitement to a store, if done right. Careful planners will watch for opportunities to bring in promotional merchandise and plan a sale around it. Save some of your open-to-buy dollars and go into the market mid-season to get some good buys so that you can have a genuine sale of merchandise while it's still hot. If you buy smart, you can take your regular markup on the price you pay and still beat the competition. Advises Widney, "You'll want to line up well ahead of time outlets that supply merchandise your customers will like at a substantial discount and deliver it promptly." He says the secret for success is to have a sale of timely items that other stores are still selling at regular prices.

No matter when you schedule your sale and what merchandise you're going to feature, you should build each sale around a theme. It should be one that can be promoted easily and can be applied throughout the store. Give a little thought to the themes you'll use. To attract the most attention, try to make them original or unusual and appropriate for your store. The actual theme isn't as important as the fact that there is one. Working with a theme usually results in a well-coordinated sale that yields added profits.

William H. Bolen, in his textbook *Contemporary Retailing* (Prentice-Hall, 1982) offers these ideas for monthly sales promotions: January, After-Christmas Sale; February, Washington's Birthday, Valentine's Day or Early Bird Spring sale; March, Easter Sale or Winter Clearance; April, After-Easter or Get-Ready-for-Summer sale; May, Mother's Day, Graduation, or Bridal promotions; June, Father's Day or Vacation sale; July, Firecracker Sale or Christmas in July; August, Back to School or Summer Clearance; September, Labor Day or Autumn sale; October, Columbus Day; November, Turkey Day or Christmas Layaway sale; December, End-of-Year Clearance or Exchange-It sale.

Often your overall marketing objectives will require that you address a special message to a particular group of your customers. Sales promotions can deliver these messages better than advertising. For example, a sales promotion can be designed to cater to customers on your mailing list. Such promotions can stimulate store visits, perhaps, or encourage shopping on certain days of the week.

You may even want to use a promotion to increase sales of fresh seasonal merchandise. Perhaps you're featuring wool suits in an autumn promotion. Send an announcement to each person on your mailing list that she will receive a gift-- say a blouse--with the purchase of a wool suit on a certain day. Or perhaps a suit purchase will make her eligible to win a free trip, or dinner at an elegant restaurant.

Exactly what will you include in your sale, whether it be a price-reduction or a seasonal promotion? It seems somewhat simplistic to say the merchandise you put on sale should be what your customers want. But that is the fact.

You'll ruin your store's image if you feature a group of low-class merchandise to which you wouldn't normally give display space. You may attract a large number of shoppers to this event, but when it's over, they'll be off to find bargains elsewhere. And your regular customers, thinking you've downgraded your stock, may transfer their loyalty to another store.

So the items shoppers will find at every sales promotion you hold must be consistent with your store image. It will be of the quality they've grown to expect from you. And it will fill the needs and tastes of the customers you've courted ever since you opened your doors.

An article in the January 1987 issue of *Sales and Marketing Management* offers these tips for creating successful sales promotions and reducing risk of failure:

1. Add value to the basic product, don't discount it.

2. Brand your sales. Make them them exclusive to you.

3. Focus on the future. Look for repeat business.

4. Theme your sales to help reinforce your advertising.

5. Look for ways to reward your best customers.

6. Look for ways to make your customers feel good about you.

7. Present your sales in a first-class way. It's worth the extra expense.

8. Make all your sales exciting and rewarding for your staff.

9. Make your sales fun and easy to execute.

Always remember that the right sale has two goals: to increase your profits and—more important—to please your customers.

Chapter Seventeen:
HOW TO FASHION
A WINNING SHOW

"Having a professional produce your fashion show eliminates many of the heartaches you can run into," says Ian Ashley, "and makes a difference that's obvious." The owner of Les Mannequins, Ltd., Hollywood fashion show coordinators, Ashley insists, "It's easy to spot the show that was professionally produced. It'll run more smoothly, have fewer hitches."

Since she's been operating her business for eight years, Ashley knows what makes a good show and what problems can crop up. She knows, too, what women like to see when they attend fashion shows.

"There are three basic kinds of fashion shows," she explains, "tearoom, ramp, and nightclub." She adds, "Both ramp and tearoom can be good for apparel stores, depending on how much merchandise you want to show and how much you want to spend."

If you're going to sponsor a show by yourself, Ashley advises, it should probably be a tearoom show and include only seven or eight garments. "If you try to show more than that, the show will be too long," she points out, since the models in a tearoom show talk with shoppers at their tables to discuss the selling points of the clothing.

Tearoom managers like to have fashion shows as entertainment, according to Ashley, and so they usually don't charge for the use of their facilities. However, the host retailer will have to really work to make sure that the show is well attended by the store's clients. Newspaper ads, phone calls, and hand-addressed invitations are good ways to get a large turnout.

A ramp show, on the other hand, does best when it's sponsored by three or four retailers in a mall or shopping center. Because such special events attract shoppers, it's likely no charge will be levied for the use of an auditorium or stage area within the mall. And sometimes your production will be promoted as part of the mall's publicity, at no cost to you.

Team up with stores that aren't direct competitors, Ashley suggests. One store provides furs, for example, and one offers bridal and evening gowns. Active sportswear might be the selection of another sponsor and business outfits still another. Audiences love a wide range of garments and using several sponsors will provide that variety without overtaxing the resources of any one store.

Once you've decided to stage a fashion show and who will sponsor it with you, you should select a theme that will define the presentation. "Back to School" and "Spring" are two often-used themes, but with a little thought you should be able to conceive a less overworked one. "Up, Up, and Away" might be effective for a show that features cruise and resort styles. "Ring in the New" could serve for a showing of new-season fashions calculated to beat the doldrums that usually follow the winter holidays. Or you could link your show to some event that's taking place in your community or area. Southern California's May Company, for example, often ties fashion promotions to special exhibits at the Los Angeles County Museum of Art. Your show coordinator is likely to have a rich supply of theme ideas, so you might want to hire him or her before you make that decision.

What are some other chores you can expect the coordinator to perform for you? Ian Ashley says, "I'll consult with the store owners about which garments to include in the show; I'll find out what features of each garment they want to play up and include that information in the show commentary, which I'll write." She notes that her major in college was English, so she's well equipped to do all writing necessary for the success of your show. That may not be true of every person who produces fashion shows, however. It's a task that calls for special skills, so you would be wise to verify a producer's claim to be able to write your commentary and publicity.

To locate someone to help you plan your fashion show--or do most of the work for you--look in the yellow pages under "Fashion show producers." You should be able to find someone who'll do as much or as little as you want.

Ian Ashley says her service also includes arranging for the hall or tearoom, chairs, ramps, microphones and other necessary equipment. She lines up music and lighting, models, and commentator, too.

There is a price for all this service, of course, and Ashley's fee starts at about $400 and rises depending on how many chores you want her to perform. It's likely that in areas less flashy than Hollywood you'll find costs to be considerably lower. But before you hire a coordinator, talk to several to learn exactly what services they perform and how much it will cost. You may find you'll want to make most of the arrangements yourself and limit the coordinator's involvement largely to advice.

On the other hand, if you're cohosting the show with two or three retailers, you may feel you can afford your share of a totally professional production. "It'll be really glamorous," says Ashley, "and well worth the expense."

Section IV:
DOING YOUR
OWN ADVERTISING

Chapter Eighteen:
WHAT NEWSPAPERS CAN DO FOR YOU

"Women," says a Crown Zellerbach Corporation advertisement, "shop twice for the clothing they buy. First in the newspapers and then in the stores." In fact, when shoppers were asked where they find information about what they're planning to buy, three out of four said they rely on ads in newspapers. And, according to the U.S. Census Bureau, about eighty percent of all adult Americans read daily newspapers.

But how can you most effectively communicate with this audience? By choosing wisely the paper in which to place your ads--and where in that paper they will appear. If yours is a town with only one newspaper, you have no option but to advertise in it. Since your competitors' ads will appear in the same paper, your challenge will be to make your ads more effective than theirs.

If, on the other hand, your store is in an area where newspapers compete for readers' attention, you'll want to learn a great deal about those readers. First, you must discover not only how many people read each paper, but also who those readers are.

Someone on the staff of a newspaper should be able to answer your questions. The *Los Angeles Times*, for example, will do demographic studies of the various areas of their circulation to help you decide which edition of their paper will get the best results for you. "We can tell retailers the mix of people they'll be reaching," says John Jenkins, advertising account executive for the *Times*. "And we can give them a profile of our readers."

According to Mike Richards of BBDO-Los Angeles, a national advertising agency, if you're choosing between a paper that has paid circulation and one that is distributed free, you should select the one whose readers pay for it. While ads in a "throw-away" paper are better than none at all, ads in a paid-circulation publication will probably get better results because, Richards points out, "People feel if they've paid for the paper, they've got to read it."

On what days to run your ads is a little harder to determine. John Jenkins recommends that you pick days when circulation is greatest. "Food advertising day is a good one," he says, "because a lot of people buy the paper that day just to read grocery ads." Mike Richards says advertising on Sunday is always a good deal because most readers spend more time with the paper on Sundays and circulation is usually higher.

No matter what day you select, "Advertising should be continuous," say Harold Shaffer and Herbert Greenwald in the book *Independent Retailing*. A series of smaller ads, according to the experts, is far more effective than an occasional big one. In addition, regularly placed ads usually earn you lower rates.

Where in the paper should your ad appear? Many experts advise apparel stores to use the women's pages and sporting goods and computer stores to use the sports pages, but you might want to experiment by moving your ad from page to page and section to section while you weigh results. During this period of experimentation, you'll want to survey your customers to learn exactly which position commands the most attention.

Budget considerations may force you to let the newspaper's staff decide where you ad goes. ROP (run of the paper) is the usual procedure for ad placement. That means you can express a desire for a certain section or page without incurring added costs; if you specify the page or section for your ad, you'll pay as much as 50 percent extra. But, according to John Jenkins, frequent or consistent advertising can make it easier for the newspaper's make-up department to position your ad in the location you prefer.

Almost every newspaper in the land extends help to advertisers who ask for it. Some larger papers, for example, pick up and deliver advertising for their regular customers, a service smaller papers can't offer. But even the smallest publication has a creative staff–or individual–that will help you with layout and copy. They can provide artwork, too, from the illustration services they subscribe to. Some will even plan entire campaigns–if you tell them what group of readers you want to reach. Since most advertising salespeople work on a commission basis, it's money in their pockets to assist you in every possible way.

Find out, too, if the paper's editorial department will welcome news releases from you. Will they send a reporter to cover fashion shows or other special events you stage? Demographic studies, planned advertising campaigns, creative assistance, cooperation in your public relations efforts–all are services a newspaper should perform for you to establish and maintain a good working relationship.

Chapter Nineteen:
PLANNING YOUR ADS

"Successful retailing means finding a niche and filling it." As true as that often-heard adage is, it omits one important element: Potential customers must be told you've filled the niche, and advertising is your means of notification. So there's no question that you must advertise. The only questions are how much you will spend and how you will spend it.

It doesn't matter what kind of store yours is or whether you sell large sizes, active wear, or designer gowns, you start your advertising plan by deciding--realistically--how much money you hope to make in the next year. One rule of thumb says you should budget for advertising from seven to ten percent of your expected annual gross, but four to six percent is about average. Try to discover what percentage similar stores in your area are spending. Your financial advisor, or a local radio station or newspaper can probably help you get that information. Then make your advertising plan, using a figure that will let you compete aggressively.

Since all advertising is the communication of a specified message to a certain group of buyers, you must decide what message you want to send and to whom. In other words, who are you, what are you selling, and to whom are you selling it?

If yours is a budget store selling low-price apparel to blue-collar women, you have to make a lot of sales to reach your earnings goal. Your need for ads, then, will be great. You'll want to keep your store's image of no-nonsense low prices in the public eye. You'll probably have to find at least one medium (probably the local newspaper) that you can afford to utilize several times each week. It may even be that the neighborhood shopper will be the place for your ads. You'll probably also want to announce your sales on local radio stations.

If your store is at the opposite end of the spectrum--say, a vendor of exclusive designer fashions--you need to sell fewer garments to attain your financial goal, and so need to run fewer ads. A very up-scale medium is what you want to carry your message of elegance and personal service. A local magazine, classy Sunday newspaper supplement, or direct mail should be your choice.

It's more likely, however, that yours is a store that features moderate-to- better or better items, with lots of services and a special fillip that sets you apart from all the others. Perhaps you merchandise for executives or college women, or upscale professionals. That distinction is what you want to emphasize, regularly and in ways that appeal to your target customers while projecting the store image you've created.

Start shaping your campaign by figuring how many ads you'll need for your two annual clearances. Then, using actual sales figures or estimates, calculate what portion of your yearly sales are attributable to seasonal events such as Mother's Day, Christmas, Easter, and so on. Earmark the same portion of your budget for advertising during those times. Subtract all these amounts from your total planned expenditure for advertising.

The amount you have left is what you should spread evenly through the rest of the year, for both newspaper and radio ads. TV spots probably aren't a good idea for you, unless you operate a sizeable chain of stores across the coverage area of the television channel. And even then, TV will be effective only if your target audience is women who are daytime viewers. Prime time is too expensive even on local channels for small retailers to use profitably.

Much of this advertising should be of the prestige variety, ads that tell current and potential customers why they should shop at your store, more than just what they should buy. It's likely that most of the ads will be in newspapers, say on Sundays or grocery days. The radio spots you buy should be on a station whose audience fits exactly your customer profile. Your spots will be most effective if they air during "drive" or "commute" time, since it's likely most of your customers go to work or school. Evening spots don't do well because they have to compete with TV.

Spend a lot of time talking with the representatives of local radio stations and newspapers before you spend a dime. Learn what days will give you the most readers of your print ads and what hours have the most radio listeners of the kind you want to reach. Plan carefully the message you want to deliver, and don't depart from your budget. You'll find your advertising will be more effective than you ever dreamed possible.

Chapter Twenty:
PUTTING EXCITEMENT INTO THE MAIL

The most versatile of all advertising is direct mail. It can be sent to as few or as many people as you choose, and to precise groups you see as potential customers. Flyers, brochures, letters all can play an important role in helping you attract new customers.

The most popular direct mail piece is the personal letter. Indeed, one advertising authority has said, "The more personal the mailer the more effective it will be . . . and the more expensive." If you commit to using personal letters, try the following ways to boost their impact. Always address letters to a person, never to occupant; address the envelopes by hand; send them by first class mail, using a special-issue stamp, if possible. On the other hand, David Ogilvy, the guru of advertising, claims people don't notice the stamps on their mail and recommends that you use bulk mailing rates. You might want to test his claim by trying both to gauge which produces the best results.

One Beverly Hills apparel store mails colorful photographic postcards of new arrivals to its customers about once each month. The vendor supplies the cards; the store pays for addressing and postage. Both vendor and store benefit from such mailings, according to that store's manager.

However, direct mail pieces should be planned to attract new customers, not just keep present ones happy. The keys to accomplishing that end are creativity and ingenuity. For example, you might mail numbered sale flyers or brochures to a broad list of women in your trading area, a list of potential customers you have purchased, or one developed through contests, surveys, and other promotions. Recipients of the mailers come into your store to match the numbers on their flyers or brochures with a list posted in the store. A match means a good-sized discount on any purchase made during that visit or a special prize, depending on how much you want to spend. The trick to making this mailing successful is to include the numbers on a flyer or brochure you have already budgeted.

Design a mailing piece so the recipient will keep it and you'll reap benefits for months, instead of just days. A map of your shopping center, say, or a city bus schedule or train timetable might be posted on bulletin boards where your store name and message will be seen by many people. Perhaps a metric conversion table would be helpful for college students, or a listing of the home games of your school or city athletic teams. Be creative in coming up with some information that future customers will want to keep. After they've consulted the brochure several times--seeing your store name each time--they are very likely to visit your store.

You might want to try sending a special letter to all the members of selected clubs and church groups--organizations whose membership appears to match your customer profile--offering a gift or discount on their first visit to your store.

If you carry a large selection of party dresses, send flyers to all the students at the local college--or the seniors graduating from high schools in your area--announcing a promotion of prom and special event dresses. If active sportswear is more your style, ask several local workout centers to provide you with the names of their clients. Letters or brochures addressed to such fitness buffs are almost sure to bring many of them to you the next time they're shopping for workout gear. You might even eliminate postage expense by persuading spa owners to place your handbills or flyers in a prominent place where clients will take one.

Perhaps you've always wanted to use catalogs as mailers, but thought only big stores like Penney's and Sears can afford such devices. Ask your suppliers' representatives about producing catalogs of their lines, then printing your store logo on the cover. You may be pleasantly surprised at how little it will cost. Catalogs can be particularly effective for Christmas, Mother's Day, Valentine's Day, and similar special shopping seasons.

With some concentrated creative thinking, you're sure to come up with at least a dozen different ways to use mailers. But how do you develop lists of people to receive them? One effective method is to ask the local power and phone companies to give you the names and addresses of people who request service. A letter of introduction or a welcoming flyer sent to new residents of your area are sure to produce new customers.

Read all the newspapers in your trading area closely for the names of couples announcing their engagement. Then send the brides-to-be letters of congratulation and offers to help with trousseau garments or dresses for the mother of the bride or groom.

Make sure that when a shopper pays by check you add the name and address on the check to your mailing list. Ask local travel agencies for the names of their clients who are booking cruises, then include those travelers on your mailing list when you promote vacation wardrobes.

The ways to build mailing lists are almost as varied as the ways to use mailers. Just be sure the flyers, brochures, or catalogs you put in the mail are consistent with your store image and are addressed to true potential customers. You'll find well-designed mailers sent to carefully chosen recipients can have a dramatic effect on your profits.

Chapter Twenty-one:
DESIGNING A MAILER
THAT DELIVERS

Dozens of mailing pieces confront your potential customers each day; most of them are tossed into the trash, unread. How can you improve the odds in favor of your mailer? By creating one that is a blend of sparkling copy, an attractive layout, and illustrations that capture your customer's interest. With these elements construct a mailing piece that addresses the physical and psychological needs of your reader-customers. Those needs include the entire range of human desires and emotions: independence, importance, self-image, health, wealth, security, happiness, and so on.

Decide which emotion mailer will appeal to before you write even a headline. Consider something like "Red . . . It's Not for Everyone," a headline that appeals to curiosity, snobbery, and independence, emotions that often influence apparel-buying decisions. Or you may want to dramatize a different attribute of the product, exaggerating only a little: "Fluid Lines That Fool Your Scale." If you concentrate on the emotions you want to arouse, you headline will almost write itself.

With the headline (and major premise of your mailer) in mind, make a list of the other attributes you plan to advertise. What benefits do those attributes offer your potential customer? List those benefits, too. They are the selling points of your copy. Before you start writing, number these points by order of importance. They should appear in your copy with the most important ones first.

It's clear that most customers don't want to read your direct mail, no matter how short the message. So your copy must be easy to understand, show respect for you customer, appeal to her senses, and still be short enough to hold her interest.

How long should the copy be? Just long enough to answer the questions "Why buy it?" "Why buy it now?" and "Why buy it from your store?" Resist the temptation to be clever, to use a fancy phrase you saw in someone else's ad. Write in your own words, as if you were trying to convince a friend of the value of the merchandise. As you write, remember the maxim of all good writers: "Show, don't tell." Don't *say* a dress is well made, *show* the high-quality features, such as over-edged seams or a deep hem.

Keep your tone warm and friendly, informal, but not chatty, varying it slightly with the type of merchandise you're presenting. You won't want to use exactly the same voice to announce a clearance of handbags that you'd use to describe a newly arrived shipment of French lingerie, for example. However, you want your copy to represent your store.

How can you tell if what you've written says it's from your store and no other? Go over the copy, deleting your store's name, and see if it could be used for most of your competitors. If it could, rewrite it. Your ad must project the image of your store--uniquely.

Now, glance at your copy quickly. Does what you can read in about five seconds make you want to read the entire mailer? If not, rewrite it. When the copy passes this test, ask someone not connected with your business to read it. If that outsider doesn't understand it, rewrite. Never assume that your customer knows why a feature is important; explain in simple terms, avoiding jargon.

The final test of your copy is a check to make sure it creates a sense of urgency. If you're advertising coats, for example, try something like "Winter will be here sooner than you think. Select your coat today so you'll be warm on that first frosty morning." No matter what merchandise you're promoting, or the tone of your mailer, somewhere in the copy you must include a command to action: "Do it today!" "Visit us soon for best selection." "Return the coupon now." State an ending date for an offer, or "Only 25 clock-radios at this price." In other words, give a reason for action now.

When you're sure the copy is the best you can possibly do, it's time to plan the layout of the piece, a layout that projects an image of quality--like your store itself-- by being clean and uncluttered. While it's true that white space is a powerful tool in designing effective ads, the elements of your mailer--illustrations, headline, copy--shouldn't be separated by too much white space. To achieve an elegant look with lots of open space, move all the elements toward the center and let the margins be larger.

The typeface you select is important to the success of your mailer, too. Use only a single type style; more than one can lead to the cluttered look you're trying to avoid. Ask your printer to show you the styles available and help you pick the one that conveys the image you seek. Don't divide your mailing piece into a lot of confusing boxes. If you must have ruled lines between blocks of copy, use thin ones; well-phrased subheads will usually accomplish the same task more effectively, however. Since the purpose of a layout is to attract favorable attention, your mailing piece must look fresh and different from all the others in the day's mail. The object is to present your sales message clearly, using illustrations to support that message. Get readers' attention with a headline or illustration, then fulfill its promise with a subhead or first paragraph of the copy. When laying out a large piece, put your illustrations beside the main copy block; in a smaller one, put the copy entirely above or below the illustration. Never break up copy blocks with illustrations.

Should you use drawings or photos for illustration? Photos win hands down for accuracy of representation, but be sure there is action, motion, and dimension in every photograph. Surround a piece of static merchandise with props that make it appear about to be used. If a garment is shown on a model, let the model look as if she's just stopped moving, or is about to start. Try to use models who are roughly the same age as the customers you want to attract.

Should you do your mailer in color or black and white? There is no hard-and-fast rule about which is most effective. Color is particularly valuable when used to illustrate a colorful product, or in a promotion using color as an attention-getting device, such as the "Red . . . It Isn't for Everyone" headline mentioned earlier. In general, however, use color only if it adds to the visual appeal of the merchandise or the impact of the mailer. Black and white might be a wise choice in a sale announcement, because it implies economy and, hence, better buys. On the other hand, while color costs more to use, it also projects an image of elegance and quality.

One alternative that is always a bad choice is the use of just two or three colors. If your message isn't appealing in black and white, a color headline or background isn't going to improve it. And it's not worth the extra expense to put your store name or logo in a second color. Either use black and white or go all out with four-color, lifelike illustrations. You might, however, consider using color on one side, black and white on the other.

To guarantee that your direct mail pieces won't be regarded as junk mail, choose wisely from the many options available to you: Black-and-white illustrations or color; type size and layout; tone of voice of your copy. All are critical to the success of your mailer. Give each element the consideration it deserves, and you will have created a direct mail piece that projects the correct image of your store and brings enthusiastic response from your customers.

Chapter Twenty-two:
THE GOALS
OF ADVERTISING

The goals of advertising are many: to define a store's personality, to indicate its place in the community, to build its name, to stress the virtues of shopping in that store, to announce sales and promotions as well as new arrivals, to sell a product and promote an image. Ads must also build traffic, win new customers, and cater to long-standing accounts. It's not surprising, then, that it takes several kinds of ads to do the right job for your store.

Advertising experts say that every retail ad sells both a specific product and the store carrying it. But ads that concentrate directly on selling a store's image are called, rightly enough, "institutional" or "image" ads.

A recent magazine ad for the American Express card demonstrates the concept and is one you could copy, using a prominent resident of your community clad in an elegant outfit you feature and pushing the idea that women of good taste patronize your store. That ad shows a black-and-white photograph of Helen Hayes, first lady of the theater, holding a bouquet of roses. A single line of copy beneath the picture says, "Helen Hayes. Charter Cardmember since 1958." The photo shouts "quality," showing as it does a highly respected member of our society clad in classy black relieved by a single strand of pearls. The implication is that people of good taste "never leave home without it."

Another recent institutional ad that you could adapt to promote your store's image is a full newspaper page production for Nordstrom's department store. Just a few words of copy deliver the message that here is a store that cares about our country and its people. The copy, run for the Fourth of July, ends with the words, "We are proud to salute our fellow Americans." The appeal to patriotism, used subtly, is always good for a store's image.

Your store and your product merge in an image ad. The product is the store name, its personality, the fact that it is a leader in fashion and quality, that it is part of the community. These characteristics become selling points and are expressed as benefits for customers. The services you offer, the complete selection you feature, even a new line or redecorated department can be main selling points in an image ad.

One of the most often-used ad types today is the one that relies on an illustration (usually a photo) to tell a story while pushing the product. Anne Klein II ads are a memorable example of the genus.

Fieldcrest has done one of the best of recent years. It is a narrow ad running the full length of a magazine page. Black and white, it shows designer sheets knotted together, flung over a wall, and clutched by a pair of hands. The headline, "Endless beginnings / Escape from the mundane. Fashions for bed and bath." The entire concept of an escape is developed by the drawing; it's a new and unusual pitch for linens, one that you might easily adapt, especially to travel fashions.

Remember "I dreamed I went dancing in my Maidenform Bra"? In both print media and TV those ads spoke of women's new place in society, as well as in a Maidenform, a knockout campaign that wouldn't be difficult for you to reshape to your store's needs. Bali is running a similar campaign right now featuring what appear to be paintings of women clad only in Bali lingerie. By comparing the Maidenform ads with those for Bali, you may find inspiration for adapting the concept to your store's needs.

Recently, magazines have been running an especially compelling ad of the photo/story variety. It shows a father sharing an old-fashioned bathtub with his baby. The copy says merely "Pure & Natural / Feels mild, gentle, never dry. / The Gentle Clean." And yet the whole change in what people expect of fathers, how women's lives have changed, the new look families have acquired . . . all are expressed in an ad containing about ten words and a photo. It should sell the soap, too, because it shows that fathers of the new age insist on soap that is gentle for babies, pleasant to use, and natural.

Direct mail is the most versatile of ad types and the postcard is one of the most effective forms of mailed ads. It doesn't have to be opened to catch the recipient's eye and hence avoid being discarded unread; it can be as simple as a few lines of type or as complex as a color photo of new merchandise.

Space limitations make it vital that you plan postcards carefully and limit their use to specific needs. Don't try to list all the items you'll have on sale at your January clearance, for example, but do send postcards to your regular customers announcing the start of the sale, how long it will last, and perhaps any gimmicks you're planning. You might want to invite charge customers to "courtesy days," a day or two before the general public is informed--through newspaper ads--that the sale is about to start.

Photos of new merchandise may stimulate enough business to be worth their cost if you have a number of items in a special collection that will appeal to your customers. Any promotion can benefit from postcards mailed in advance.

Once you've decided what you want the card to do, create a headline that will grab the reader's eye. NEW ARRIVALS might be one; SHOP AHEAD OF THE CROWD might be a good way to alert charge customers to a coming sale. For your semiannual clearance sale you might just write IT'S THAT TIME AGAIN / Our sixth annual summer [or winter] sale starts Monday, [the date] / Bring this card in for a favored shopper discount.

Black on white will be the least expensive color scheme for your card, but color adds excitement and prestige. You might want to try a good quality colored paper stock with black ink and one color ink on one side and black plus another color on the other side. Don't hesitate to ask your printer for price quotes on ideas you come up with and ask him to devise some of his own, keeping your budget in mind. And don't fail to confer with postal authorities about the sizes of cards you can use without needing additional postage, about mailing permits, sorting requirements, and other practical aspects of using cards.

Some of the country's best--and worst--advertising has been done on television. No apparel retailer could forget the famous 501 jeans ads that told stories, almost ignoring the jeans and taking it for granted that everyone will buy Levi's at one time or another.

A similar campaign produced more recently is the one for Jordache in which a girl whines that she hates her mother. As one critic said, "There'd be no way to tell it was a jeans commercial if it wasn't so dumb." The Jordache ads have stirred up a great deal of controversy, as have similar campaigns by Guess? and Calvin Klein. Another advertising expert wrote of TV ads that they are 60-second short stories. And when they are good, they are very good, and when they are bad, they are horrid.

On local TV, however, an ad has a chance to tell about a store and its merchandise and to show it in action. Whether it's the courteous service or new ways to tie scarves, a good TV spot can show it. Seek expert help, if not from a local advertising agency, then from TV students at a local college or university.

While most retail TV ads are strongly insititutional, any TV ad, no matter how short, must mention and show the store name: show merchandise in action, and state the selling points; restate and reshow the store name; and show and say the address and phone number, repeating it once.

Be aware, however, that most local TV advertising is so bad as to be offensive enough to drive shoppers into other stores. Insist on quality before you plunk down all the money that a TV campaign will cost.

Make sure, too, that channels you are considering have a good client/audience profile that sheds more specific light on who is in a particular TV audience, not just how many. David Poltrack, head of research at CBS says, "The current age-based demographics that advertisers focus on don't give enough weight to the differences among people within a given age group." Most TV advertising, for example, is pitched at the 25-to-49 age segment. But do 25 year olds have the same tastes, needs, and pocketbooks as 49 year olds? In fact, TV often treats people over 50 as an unwanted audience, even though that is the group that has the most disposable income. So investigate before you spend large sums on TV ads.

You probably haven't thought of it that way, but the sign that says, "Sweaters–$14.95" is an ad.   Any poster or notice you put in your window or even on the selling floor is supposed to accomplish at least some of the goals of advertising.

Window banners are especially important since they attract customers that aren't on your mailing list and may not read local newspapers. You probably don't need to be told to put signs in the window for a sale, but consider the store that fills its window with mannequins swathed in banners proclaiming, "Semiannual clearance." Think how much more attention such a tactic will capture than a simple sign.

One aspect of in-store advertising that many retailers neglect is tying it in with media ads. If your ads contain catch-phrases (the Maidenform campaign comes to mind again) use the same phrases in signs and posters in the store. The main trick to bear in mind is that these messages must be brief. Shoppers walking by seldom stop to read a long pitch. About 15 words is supposed to be the most passersby can read and comprehend.

When it comes to store placards, they should be planned to get shoppers into the store, nothing else. During a sale HUGE DISCOUNTS may be statement enough, but not if every other store in the mall is saying the same thing. Consider something like IF YOU SHOP HERE FIRST, YOU'LL SHOP HERE LAST. That's brief enough to be read in passing and implies a great deal.

You must be careful not to let posters and banners in the store destroy the image of quality you've built with your ads. Don't, for example, let your nephew letter signs with his Christmas crayons. Have them painted professionally or do it yourself, using alphabet stencils.

Brand names are good material for store posters and banners. If your store design allows shoppers to see in as they pass, it may be they'll discover you carry a brand they favor. Voila! They come in to shop.

In-store advertising should also trigger impulse buying. A tasteful sign on the wall behind the cash register, for example, or a sign on an easel near the dressing rooms can have terrific impact. Perhaps pictures of some of your photogenic customers in outfits they've purchased from you might be a good in-store ad. You might give the amateur models a big discount from the merchandise to persuade them to pose.

Be imaginative in creating these signs and in-store ads; they can be extremely forceful and cost very little, compared to other media. Just be careful that they are always low-key and in good taste. Exactly like most of your other ads, they should whisper, not shout, "Buy me, buy me here, buy me now."

SECTION V:
BUYING

Chapter Twenty-three:
HOW TO LOCATE
NEW RESOURCES

Finding vendors who can supply attractive merchandise at competitive prices is a strenuous, time-consuming chore, but it's one that is critical to the continued success of your business. In fact, reliable suppliers are so highly prized that many buyers keep their files of vendor information locked in the safe along with cash and other valuables. Having contact with a variety of vendors is particularly important if the styling and quality of some vendors' lines are likely to vary from one season to the next. You need also to develop ways to make sure the merchandise you stock is always fresh and innovative, yet appealing to the customers you want to attract. How can you develop a list of resources that you can rely on to supply you with good merchandise, deliver it when promised and settle claims promptly, while offering good credit terms and advertising allowances?

"It takes a lot of legwork," says Barbara of the Beautiful Web in Beverly Hills. "You have to walk the mart," she explains. Harry Boschier of G. B. Harb and Sons in Los Angeles, agrees, saying, "Either the mart or the clothing shows themselves, in New York or Los Angeles."

Boschier is quick to add, however, that his store does much of its ordering from sales representatives who call on them. Most of them have catalogs, he notes, saying, "If we know the product or have used the merchandise before, we order from catalogs. But I'd be afraid to order cold. We're into pure fabrics like cotton, silk, and wool," he goes on, "so I'd like to see the fabric before I ordered. But I've ordered belts and accessories and things from in-stock catalogs."

Laurie Boede, buyer for Draper's and Damon's of Pasadena, says, "Most buyers don't have enough time to develop new resources, scouting them out and researching them." She adds, however, that from marts and shows you can get lists of vendors whose representatives you can ask to call on you. "But," she advises, "shop other stores, making note of what customers are reacting to. Check the labels of garments you're interested in and then contact the manufacturer." One authority on retailing says, "Visit a Nieman-Marcus whenever you have a chance." Laurie Boede offers what would seem to be an almost obvious tip for stores that pride themselves on personal service: "Talk to your customers, too. Find out if they've seen something they like by a manufacturer you don't deal with."

These buyers and the authors of many textbooks on retailing agree that a search for suppliers should be done on a systematic basis. Make a list of the various means you'll try, then explore one of them each time you have a few free minutes.

The first item on your list should be trade magazines such as *Women's Wear Daily*. Read both articles and ads, looking for names of new vendors. Contact any you find of interest and ask them to have a representative call on you.

Read *Vogue* and *Seventeen* and other fashion magazines, too. Again, study both articles and advertisements to discover what's hot and who supplies it. Many magazines have at the back of the publication a column of ordering information from which you can glean vendors' names. Or call any phone number appearing in the ads and ask for details about the supplier. Your reading research, of course, should be continuous, as long as you're in the retail business.

Attend shows whenever you can. The January meeting of the National Retail Merchants Association is planned for apparel retailers and could be very helpful to you. Every other year or so, try to make it to one of the big markets in New York, Montreal, Dallas, or Los Angeles. Even if you don't plan to buy there, you'll find the trip worthwhile because of the contacts you'll make.

The final item on your strategy list might be to locate a resident buying office to represent you. A buying office representative will accompany your or your buyer on market visits to help you locate best buys. A resident buyer may also arrange for a group of suppliers to show their wares for you when you're in town.

Reporting on quality levels and dependability of suppliers is another function of resident buyers. These offices issue information on new items and price deals, and often play an important role in making group buying arrangements. They should provide a constant flow of market information in the form of letters, reports, bulletins. Many even consolidate shipments from several vendors.

A spokesperson for George Entin and Associates, a resident buying office in Los Angeles, says, "We can save the store a trip to Los Angeles." She adds that they supply catalogs if the owner requests them from specific manufacturers, but they don't routinely send out flyers or tips sheets, as do most offices. "If there's a problem with an order," the Entin representative says, "we smooth it out." Eliminating such snags as misordered merchandise, late shipments, and necessary adjustments are just some of the ways a buying office can make life easier for you.

Very small stores usually pay a flat fee for the services of a buying office, since a percentage of orders placed might not be adequate payment for so many services.

It could be that the cost would outweigh the benefits you'll reap, but check it out with some of the resident buying offices listed in your yellow pages. A steady supply of new and exciting suppliers could very well be worth the expense.

Plan a campaign for attacking the problem of locating new resources. You're sure to find enough of them to make the time and effort expended worthwhile.

Chapter Twenty-four:
HOW TO BUY
SUPERSTAR FASHIONS

Are you thinking you'd like to stock a few pieces from Anne Klein II, say, or Liz Claiborne to upgrade your store's image? Have you even made a few stabs at placing an order with one of the fashion superstars only to be put off by some snooty sales rep? Well, don't be intimidated into thinking you're not good enough or big enough to carry one of the high-priced, big-name lines. If you have a good credit rating, you may be able to pull it off by yourself. You certainly can accomplish such an order through a buying group or resident buyer.

Some resident buyers who haven't had a great deal of experience in buying from the "biggies" have themselves been intimidated. A buyer in Los Angeles, for example, says, "They don't want specialty store business; they want department stores." She adds that you have to be approved to buy Anne Klein II, that they have to inspect your store, have pictures of it to guarantee that yours is the kind of store they want to feature their labels.

A spokeswoman for the Jan Biederman buying office in Los Angeles, says the big-name fashion houses set very high minimum purchase requirements to discourage small stores. But it is possible to order from them, she says. It's usually done through some kind of showroom.

Sally Donahue, another L.A. resident buyer, says the apparel superstars aren't inaccessible, you just have to know how to reach them. "I take the 12 minimum order," she says, "and write it under one store's name." She adds that all participating stores share freight costs of the consolidated order. She also points out that not as many manufacturers have huge minimum order quantities, anymore. "They all want to sell their merchandise," she notes.

Sid Clayman, an off-price resident buyer in Los Angeles, says, "Huge minimums are a rarity, today. Most of them have been lowered." He advises that you consult buying offices in New York until you find one that has the buying power and reputation needed to deal with resources that might be prima donnas. He says, "I can go to any resource that I've done business with in the past and write individual orders for each of my accounts. They don't have to consolidate and reship." He points out that he represents both small, single-store operations and huge chains that do $200 to $300 million in business each year.

Clayman points out, too, that some of the big fashion houses "dump" merchandise when they become inundated with inventory that hasn't sold. A representative in the east, he says, handles all Liz Claiborne goods that are disposed of in such a fashion. Surplus inventory is first offered to the manufacturer's regular clients, then to big off-price chains--Marshall's, for example--and, finally, to jobbers. If you're interested in stocking fashion superstars' overproduction, you just have to stay in touch with the markets so that you'll be informed when such merchandise is available.

On the other hand, if it's brand new, current season merchandise you want to order from one of the famous houses, it's no big deal, according to Joe Siegel, vice president of merchandising of the National Retail Merchants' Association. All the manufacturer really wants is for you to pay your bill on time. So, if you've got a good credit rating, you can buy from any of them.

Some of them, he says--noting that Liz Claiborne is the only one that does this in a major way--some of them insist that you buy packages of their goods, not individual items. One of the reasons for that, he explains, is that Claiborne has 26 factories scattered all over the world. In order to turn out merchandise at the price she does, she prepackages all of her groups and stocks the cartons in distribution centers. The packages, according to Siegel, are too large for retailers with fewer than three stores. But that's where your buying group comes in, he adds.

Just look up a representative for the house you want to deal with and then go from there, Siegel urges. It's silly to be intimidated; they're delighted to sell to anyone who can pay promptly. And very few of them ask for COD payment. If they should, be sure to have cash or a cashier's check ready when the shipment arrives, he advises.

And what if the high-fashion resource insists on inspecting your store before it will accept your order? It's a common practice and done to protect them from selling to discounters. If they're selling to stores like Robinson's or I. Magnin, they don't want to lose those good accounts by having a small store knocking off prices. Also, the big houses don't want their fashions to end up on sale in a "bare walls and plain pipe racks" store. They strive to protect their quality image just as you do. So if yours is a store with a good image and you're not selling at discount prices, Siegel advises, don't be terrified by big fashion houses. Deal with them directly or locate a New York buying office that will do it for you. It's sure to be a happy experience, he says.

Chapter Twenty-five:
YOUR OWN LABEL

"It's a form of advertising," says Bruce Helft of Helft's Fine Apparel for Women, referring to the private labels that appear in many of the garments sold in his Southern California stores. "We have the labels made and supply them to our manufacturers. The additional cost is insignificant and we don't run into any real problems," he says, adding, "A customer, seeing the label, remembers she bought the dress from us and (that) it was a happy experience." Helft makes the addition of private labels sound like an easy solution to many of the problems that confront independent retailers of women's apparel.

For smaller retailers, though, private labeling may well be a good deal, but one that is a little more difficult to accomplish than Helft implies. Sarah Worman of the Fashion Institute of Los Angeles says a small independent couldn't accomplish it alone. For example, Maria Bogart, spokesperson for the two stores of Large and Beautiful Fashions, says, "We only put them in the garments we make ourselves. The ones we order carry the manufacturers' labels." But Carroll and Company of Los Angeles, a single-store operation, reports that their manufacturer puts the company's own labels in all their garments, even those ordered in fairly small quantities, with no appreciable additional expense and no difficulties. They have, however, used the same manufacturer for 35 years.

Joni Iqal, buyer for another California independent, G. B. Harb and Son, agrees private labels are "Nice to have. They make each purchase a little more personal and show that the customer is buying quality merchandise." She adds, however, that only about 20 percent of their women's clothing is so identified. Explaining that their store also handles men's wear, she notes that more manufacturers of men's clothing seem willing to perform that special service for retailers. "But almost all of our women's sweaters have our private label," she says, pointing out that it's the more traditional manufacturers who are willing to sew in labels supplied by the retailer.

No matter how labels eventually find their way into garments, they start out being made by one of many label manufacturers in the country. Harry Herz of Alcon Labels in Los Angeles says his company is the leader in the woven label industry, with five mills producing only woven, not printed, labels. "Small retailers order a supply from us every few years," he says, emphasizing that his firm charges no set-up fee and nothing additional for supplying artwork. Minimum order requirements aren't prohibitive, either. A retailer wanting to order satin labels must take at least 1,000, while the minimum order quantity for polyester is 3,000 labels. Cost for the minimum quantity of either variety will run about $650, according to Herz, who says that some of his customers are Carroll and Company and Kitty Bernharth Fashions in Beverly Hills.

Rospatch, the supplier of labels for such firms as J. C. Penney and Sears, produces both woven and printed varieties. "Minimum orders," says a spokesman for the company, "are about 1,000 labels." Rospatch takes about six weeks to fill an order, with printed labels costing under $200 for five thousand and the same number of woven satin ones costing around $225. There is no additional charge for artwork.

Still another label maker is Minkoff Associates of Los Angeles, which produces both woven labels in a number of colors and sizes, and printed ones in either polyester or cotton. Minimum orders are $650 for woven varieties and $75 for printed. This firm, too, will assist with artwork, if necessary, but it levies a one-time charge of $35 for the printing plate.

At all label-making firms, the unit price is determined by the quantity ordered. Thus, it will pay you to order the largest quantity you can handle--short of a lifetime supply. Kept under cover, where they won't become soiled, labels won't deteriorate, so there's little reason to purchase uneconomical minimum quantities.

The consensus among many independent retailers seems to be that private labels can serve as the mark of better quality apparel, that the problems attendant on using them are worth the added prestige, and that the cost--usually only a few pennies per garment--shouldn't be an important consideration.

Once you've made the decision to use your own labels, you'll want to select a design that is truly representative of your store. You might call on students of your local art school or junior college to help you produce a clean, attractive design. Or you could stage a contest among your employees with a special award for the one who comes up with the label design that best projects the store image you strive for. It's likely that this impression of quality will be easier to achieve with woven labels, rather than printed. Woven ones will stay bright, too, through many washings or dry cleanings, while the printed kind are sure to fade to illegibility long before the garment is worn out.

Locating a supplier for your labels can be as simple as looking in the yellow pages, but how do the labels you buy get sewn into the garments you sell? At Kitty Bernharth's, her employees apply labels to clothing only after it is sold. Marion Wagner, Inc., however, assigns the task of stitching in labels to the part-time employee who is responsible for pressing and steaming newly arrived garments. A representative of Marion Wagner says, "We do have a couple of manufacturers in

Italy who will put our labels in the garments we order."

Perhaps the most straightforward route to your own private labels, however, is through a buying office. Working with such a cooperative group, you can join forces with operators of stores who feature the same types of merchandise you do. Mack Davis, who is now a professor in the Entrepreneur Program of the University of Southern California, tells how he handled the problem of private labels when he was operating a retail store: "We got six stores together," he says, "stores that all sold similar types of merchandise." He says these stores were located in widely separated geographic locations: Boulder, Colorado, for example, and Norman, Oklahoma, and one in Missouri, so they weren't competing with each other. "We located sources for the things we wanted to buy, then placed large orders based on our pooled needs."

"I ran our buying group," Davis notes, "and if I saw something we might want, I'd send out flyers to the other stores. If enough of them agreed to participate, we'd be able to order a large quantity." Davis says he usually worked through a buying syndicate in New York that would find different lines as they became available. Then manufacturers would put each store's labels in the garments.

You may also want to explore the possibility of dealing directly with the manufacturer, particularly if it's one with whom you've been doing business for a long time. You may be able to convince their representative that the firm should render this service to repay you for your loyalty or your habit of paying promptly. Joni Iqal says she thinks adding labels is one enticement manufacturers can use to get your business.

Remember, though, that you won't want to put your label in every garment you stock. It should be reserved for very special items or lines, ones that will help to reinforce the image of high quality you've created. In addition, you probably won't be granted any allowance for cooperative advertising of your private labels. On the other hand, Mack Davis points out that his group would do joint labeling, if the manufacturer was offering a big advertising allowance. "You know," he says, "the label would say 'Made by XYZ Company for WWW stores.' " But that happened only rarely.

As Bruce Helft says, private labels can create a happy connection between your store and your customers' pleasure with their clothing. Design a label that's in good taste, restrict its use to a few select garments, and you've taken another giant stride toward convincing your customers that yours is a quality store that can meet all their apparel needs.

Chapter Twenty-six:
THE FLAP OVER PRIVATE LABEL

Have a couple of your favorite resources faded from the scene in the past few months? They may have fallen victim to competition presented by the growing phenomenon of private labels. For example, in the last two years the Hathaway women's line and Stanley Blacker closed down because their customers had found other suppliers, presumably better--or less expensive--ones. Carol Horn knitwear and designer collections have disappeared, too, as has Happy Legs. Dozens of other once-popular lines have fallen by the wayside.

Exactly why are all these makers of women's wear retreating? The continuing softness of the entire apparel business is at the heart of the problem, of course, but Robert D. Czwartacky, former managing director of Panther (another vanished label) says, "What's happening is those manufacturers who make a basic product have to compete with stores, who have gone into making moderate basic merchandise for themselves."

What are private labels and how do they create added competition? If you've ever bought Townhouse tomatoes or Empress grape jelly at a Safeway supermarket, you've bought a private label, not very different from the ones that are giving apparel makers fits today. For years those private brands have competed for shelf space and customers' dollars with the likes of Del Monte and Kraft. Sears has been selling its Craftsman tools, a private brand made just for the department store giant, alongside Black and Decker drills, say, or Stanley hammers for several decades.

Bruce Helft of Helft's Fine Apparel for Women, as you will remember, supplies labels to manufacturers who stitch them into garments in lieu of any other labels, so it looks as if the garments were designed and made just for his stores. And in some cases, they were. Just like the babyfood peaches that for years have been strained and packed by independent canneries to the strict requirements of Gerber, large stores and chains often order from manufacturers clothing of their own design and specifications.

In many cases, quality control seems to be as important a motive for private labeling as profits. A recent article in *PC Week* reports that Computerland is about to launch house brands. Several electronics authorities say such a move--not unlike Sears' introduction of its own brands a generation ago--was to be expected and could eventually reduce prices and improve quality. A marketing executive at Radio Shack (a prominent retailer of budget computers and equipment) says a house brand allows a chain to contract for uniform specifications. It also inspires consumers to transfer their loyalty from the manufacturer to the store selling the brand.

Small chains and even single stores have found that they can have their own private labels added to special items they order through a cooperative buying office. The cost is negligible and the impact, as some manufacturers are discovering, can be terrific.

"Private label eliminates the middlemen," says Ed Razek of the Limited. Clothes are manufactured in volume to a store's (or buying co-op's) specifications and shipped directly, bypassing showrooms, salesmen, advertising--all legitimate costs of running a retail business. Most stores see house labels as a way to maintain both profit margins and quality while offering customers lower prices. According to another recent article, this one in *Glamour*, "A cashmere sweater made in Hong Kong for $50--often in the same factories (same machinery, same skilled labor) used by a name designer--retails for $125. If that same sweater bore a designer label, intermediate fees would boost the wholesale price to $125, which the store would double to $250." In advising its readers that store brands offer the best value for their money, the article explained why: "Two linen jackets: similar style, fabric, construction, and color. One costs $225, the other $125. What's the difference? Check the label. Chances are the $225 jacket has a brand name while the less expensive version bears the name of the store."

Thus, designer brands now have another layer of competition to face. And this one is creating some degree of consternation in the apparel trade. Consider the plans of Carter Hawley Hale, the Los Angeles-based department store that *Fortune* labels a "plain-jane retailer." Writing in that publication Bill Saporito says CHH is now "spiffing up old-fashioned department stores with snappy merchandise and service."

After spinning off Bergdorf Goodman and Neiman-Marcus in late 1987, CHH was left with five department store chains catering to middle-income customers, who have been doing more and more of their shopping at off-price or specialty stores. To start the redesign process, and win back those customers, CHH officials will, first and foremost, push service. As we hear so often, any store that is experiencing some kind of trouble should first examine closely the kind of service it offers.

To sharpen its fashion image, however, CHH will join the latest trend and boost its private-label business. The firm is just beginning to catch up in private-label selling. By manufacturing goods and selling them under its own labels, the company can create cachet for items available nowhere else, while capturing the profits of both distributor and retailer.

Not all a store's stock should bear its private label. And, because it takes a certain amount of volume to keep prices low, if you decide to cash in on the private label boom, you'll probably limit the collection to a smaller range of colors and sizes.

Don't be misled; private label is not a brand new idea in the fashion world, just an old one coming back to popularity. Department stores have always sold goods "made expressly" for Macy's, or whomever, but the growing popularity of designer names such as Ralph Lauren or Calvin Klein has made the retailing giants take another look at such labeling.

How did they attack the problem? To put it bluntly, by fooling the customer. Says Mark Handler, president of R. H. Macy & Co., "Now we try to make the brands look like individual manufacturers'." In other words, these days, they slap made-up designer names on the labels they have sewn into garments they order. For example, Marshall Field's sells its own lingerie under the Victorian name of Amelia's; Saks Fifth Avenue calls its women's career clothing the Works, while Macy's tags its rugged weekend gear Aeropostale. The Limited's Forenza sportswear is an outstanding example of a made-up, foreign-sounding designer name. You'll even find such private labels in catalogs, always with the notation, "Exclusively ours."

Does the private label work for these biggies? "You bet," says Susan Caminiti, writing in *Newsweek*. "Some 30 percent of Macy's total sales come from its private labels, and its most popular brand, Charter Club, a collection of moderately priced women's apparel and accessories, rings up annual sales of more than $100 million." It's one way an independent can gain an advantage over the big-name manufacturer, building customer loyalty for a brand they can buy only in your store. Says industry consultant Emanuel Weintraub, "When everything else looks the same in the stores, private label lets a retailer have a certain degree of exclusivity."

Chapter Twenty-seven:
GETTING MERCHANDISE WHEN YOU NEED IT

No matter how carefully you selected the merchandise the last time you placed an order, no matter how much retailing savvy helped you make decisions, your work was all in vain unless the items you contracted for are on your sales floor exactly when you need them. Say you ordered plaid skirts from one resource and complementary blazers from another, both to star in your back-to-school promotion. How can you be sure they'll arrive, not just at the same time, but when you need them? What do you do if the blazers arrive late and the skirts have sold out? You're left with a bunch of blazers that go with nothing in your stock. Or perhaps you've ordered an exciting selection of swimsuits. What will you do with them if they arrive two weeks after your swimsuit promotion ends?

"It's pretty tough at the small specialty store level," says Andrea Weeks, merchandise planning and control instructor at the Los Angeles Fashion Institute. But she (like the Small Business Administration and other experts) says the solution to the problem starts with your purchase order.

Have your P.O. forms printed if you can afford the expense. If not, be sure to include on every order a phrase such as, "No partial orders or late shipments accepted." Show the name and address of the vendor, a good description of the merchandise, the price you agreed to pay and terms of payment. You'll need to show the date the order is entered with the vendor (to make follow-up easier) and a specific date for delivery. Never use "as soon as possible." Show what shipper will be used, routing if needed, and who will pay freight costs. It isn't good practice, according to the SBA, to tell a vendor to use the "best way" to ship. Finally, show your tax identification number.

According to Jim Dixon of RMSA (Retail Merchandising Service Automation, Inc.), both early and late deliveries can throw your best merchandise plans awry. Fashion merchandise, especially, he says, should start arriving 30 days before a new season. As the season proceeds, the inflow of merchandise tapers off and stocks for the following season start to arrive. Maximum sales and minimum markdowns depend on the arrival of merchandise as scheduled.

On the other hand, merchandise displayed too far in advance of the season becomes old in customers' eyes before they are ready to buy it. When goods arrive late, the limited time left for selling it results in excess markdowns at season's end. Avoiding these pitfalls comes from requiring vendors to honor the terms specified on your purchase order.

Once an order is placed, file one copy of the P.O. in your tickler file. Two months before the delivery date, on the first and fifteenth of that month, call the vendor to verify that the shipment is scheduled. Do the same thing the month before shipment, and again a week before the ship date. Then, two or three days after the shipment date, call the vendor and ask for a bill of lading, number of packages, and weight of shipment. "I'm not saying wholesalers lie," says Andrea Weeks, "but if they tell you, 'Yeah, it's been shipped,' be sure it's true. And," she adds, "if you're told the shipment comprises only one package weighing a couple of pounds, you know you've been short shipped."

Weeks advises, if you receive only a portion of your order, that you send it back saying, "This is not what we agreed on. Therefore we will not accept any part of it." She points out that you're really worse off having a part of the order because they'll ship the other part later, and then you never have your entire collection at one time. "Say that you accept a partial shipment," she says, "and it sells. Since you've accepted a portion of the order incorrectly shipped, you're in a very bad position to refuse the rest of the order that now doesn't fit in with the rest of your stock." Weeks notes that you must be firm about any departure from terms you specified on your order. "Cancel the entire order," she advises, "and make the wholesaler see that it's to their benefit to ship your orders correctly." Once they discover you'll accept whatever they ship whenever they ship it, they'll handle your orders last.

However, a cancellation from a small store may not be as important to a resource as one from, say, Macy's. It should be effective, though, Weeks notes, if you have established a really good relationship with your resources. "Where department stores will drop vendors for no apparent reason," she says, "small stores are usually loyal. Make it plain that you'll hang in with a reliable vendor in good times and tough." Don't limit your purchases to just one or two vendors, but be consistent about placing orders with a small group of suppliers who have shown you they have quality merchandise and will deliver your orders complete and on time.

Chapter Twenty-eight:
HOW TO COPE
WITH A NIGHTMARE

You dream of it happening in your worst nightmare: Two weeks before he's supposed to ship merchandise that's a large and essential part of your spring collection, the supplier goes belly-up. What do you do now? How can you fill the gap in your merchandise? How can you make sure it never happens again?

Not even the Census Bureau can put a finger on exactly how often small manufacturers and distributors are going out of business, but most experts agree it's happening with increasing frequency. "Partly, it's because the market is so tight right now," says Dorothy Metcalfe, chairwoman of Merchandise Marketing at the Los Angeles Fashion Institute. "People are being very tight with their inventories," she says, "and not buying as much." She points out that some suppliers depend on very large orders to survive. When those big orders fail to materialize, the operator on a shoestring simply folds. Metcalfe adds, as an aside, that retailers--to make the grade in today's very volatile marketplace--must be more attuned to who their customers are, and stop trying to be all things to all people. "Really target your markets," she urges.

Getting caught short because of a failed supplier should never happen, according to Terri Coons, lecturer on retail management at the University of Southern California school of business. "You should be on top of what's coming and when," she says. "You should have known at least one or two weeks ago that there was a problem." Coons advises, "Keep track of your orders." "Verify that the shipping date will be met," Andrea Weeks, instructor of merchandise planning and control at the Los Angeles Fashion Institute says. Once an order is placed, file one copy of the P.O. in your tickler file. Two months before the delivery date, on the first and fifteenth of that month, call the vendor to verify that shipment is scheduled. Do the same thing a month before the shipment, and again a week before the ship date.

"If you're just waiting for Thursday--the day the goods are supposed to be shipped--and they don't come," says Coons, "you're not really doing your homework. You should have realized a couple of weeks ago that there was a problem." She says if you call and find the phone's been disconnected, that's a pretty good tip-off that something's wrong. If no one answers the phone when you call a month or two before the ship date, send a certified letter inquiring about the status of the shipment. Pay the extra fees required to receive a return receipt that shows by whom the letter was received, at what address, and on what date. That information should reveal if the company is still functioning. If it doesn't seem to be, and you still can reach no one on the phone, send another certified letter canceling the order so you're free to look elsewhere.

To keep this nightmare from ever becoming a reality for you, says Dr. Karen Walker, director of Fashion Marketing at Woodbury University in Burbank, California, "You might want to deal only with substantial vendors." Coons agrees, saying, "I wouldn't even do business with somebody that wasn't major, unless we're talking only one percent or so of your inventory. I wouldn't put the bulk of my merchandise into unknown hands. Choose reliable people that have a good reputation." She even advises that before you place your first order with a vendor, you visit the company, if it's close enough, to find out beforehand what kind of company you're dealing with. For example, are they just cutting goods from order to order? Check with other store owners to get an idea of the track record of each new vendor.

Once your horse is stolen (so to speak), however, it's too late to talk about locking the barn door. What do you do if it *does* come to pass that a vendor you relied on to supply the bulk of your spring collection has let you down? "That's easy!" says Terri Coons. "There's tons of merchandise out there. Make phone calls and go buy some more. There's always merchandise around." If you've been in business for some time, you should have no problem, she insists. "Unless you've been buying from only two or three people; then you could be hung out to dry." She adds, "Don't deal with too few resources; you could cut yourself short."

If you belong to a buying service, ask your representative to locate the look or specific label you need to replace. Network, too. Call friends who sell lines similar to the ones you're missing for the names of their suppliers. Prowl through the apparel departments of several major stores to find other labels with the look you need. Call the apparel mart nearest to you to locate a representative of the label you're interested in. Take a walk through the yellow pages to discover what individuals or organizations may be able to help you. Someone listed there is sure to know who can supply in a hurry the items you lack. You will probably have to scramble for a few hours, but saving your season's business is worth it.

Once the crisis is past, make sure it never happens again. Don't put all your eggs in one basket. Deal with several suppliers. If you entrust them with substantial portions of your inventory, make sure they're big enough and well enough placed to survive periods of rough business weather. Don't ever let yourself be at the mercy of a vendor; control your own business.

SECTION VI:
YOUR CUSTOMERS

Chapter Twenty-nine:
MORE THAN JUST COUNTING NOSES

Have you ever wondered how a magazine can cite with confidence the ages, incomes, and marital status of its readers? Advertising agencies, too, seem to have a crystal ball that reveals to them who is drinking wine coolers this year and who's sipping light beer. How do they do it? Could you use their techniques to draw an accurate picture of potential customers for your store?

Analysis of the social traits of a society is accomplished through demography--a branch of the science of statistics. The most common example of such data, know as demographics, is the U.S. Census, taken every ten years since 1790. Originally little more than a count of heads, the census has become a very detailed analysis of Americans and their habits. When combined with survey results, Arbitron findings, and the like, census data can be manipulated to reveal a great deal about what Americans like and dislike, how much they earn and save, what kind of work they do, even how far they travel to work.

If you like working with numbers and are good at it, you can probably analyze much of the data from the latest census yourself. You'll want to know the number of women--women of an age to shop in your store--in your target area, the lifestyles of those women, their disposable incomes (the amount they have left after taxes and other government-mandated payments). You'll want to know if these potential customers are buying and furnishing homes or if they rent their living space, how much of their total family income they spend on the types of goods you sell. The more you can figure out about the income and spending habits of shoppers in your trade area, the better you'll be able to satisfy their needs.

All this information and much more is available with some extensive digging through census publications on the shelves of nearly 2000 libraries throughout the country. Call libraries in your area until you locate one designated "a depository of government documents." Or call the nearest office of the Census Bureau for the location of the depository library most convenient for you. There you will find detailed population characteristics of your state. You should also find a subject report, "Places of Work." Together these publications can show, county by county, sex and marital characteristics, age and years of school, earnings, and other information about the population of your state and county. For help in understanding these and other Census Bureau publications contact Customer Services; Bureau of the Census; Data User Service Division; Washington, DC 20233. You may also want to invest in *Measuring Markets–a Guide to the Use of Federal and State Statistical Data*, costing about $3.75 from the Superintendent of Documents; Government Printing Office; Washington, DC 20402-9325. From the same address you can order a subscription to *data user NEWS*, a monthly publication that costs just $21 a year. It tells you where to find the statistics you need to keep up with trends; who to call for more details; where on the local scene you can turn for information; what's in the works for the Census Bureau.

It's a challenging and time-consuming chore, however, working through all this data yourself. It may prove to be more cost effective for you to use a marketing consulting firm to do the job. They are listed in your yellow pages and offer a wide variety of tools for successful market planning.

From such an organization you can obtain analyses of any geographic area you specify, such as metropolitan areas, census tracts, or zip code areas, and in as much detail as you are willing to pay for. You can request data about occupational characteristics, ages and racial background of the population, personal income (which includes a variety of nonmonetary types of income), education, number of households, and number of workers per household. A sales representative of the consulting firm you select will advise you on how to define your target area and what data will be most meaningful for you. The cost for a detailed analysis will probably be around $150. One of these companies, Urban Decision Systems, Inc., of Los Angeles and Westport, Connecticut, promises reports in just a day or two, once you've determined exactly how much data you need. Some promise even faster delivery if you have a computer terminal and a modem. You can obtain cost estimates and free information sheets, such as "Retail Potential: Individual Store Reports" or "Retail Potential: Shopping Center Reports," by calling Urban Decision Systems at (213) 820-3931 or (203) 226-8188.

If you live in a metropolitan area, your local newspaper may have already done demographic studies of this type and will make the data available to advertisers as a free or low-cost service. Some large chambers of commerce also have such studies on hand or can order them for members more economically than can individual store owners. Call both the largest paper in your area and your chamber of commerce to learn if either of them offers these services.

Television and radio stations, advertising agencies, and magazine publishers have all found it pays to study the markets and so will you. But do compare all possible sources of assistance before you commit to spending a great deal of money.

Chapter Thirty:
TAKING A CLOSER LOOK AT YOUR CUSTOMERS

You've expended a a great deal of energy (and possibly a fair sum of money, as well) to learn the demographics of your trading area. You've consulted with the chamber of commerce and your local newspaper to plan the focus of your marketing efforts. But now that you know how many local residents own their homes, how much of their paychecks they have left over to spend each month, and how old they are, do you really know them? What kind of recreation do they enjoy, for example? Is their idea of a big night out a bowling tournament, a workout at the gym, or a fancy party? Indeed, do they even go out? Or are they into "cocooning," staying home to watch movies on their VCR and ordering dinner in? Nothing in routine demographic studies will tell you about these aspects of your customers' lives. And yet it's clear that the primary goal of a retail store should be to offer its customers merchandise that fits their lifestyles.

William R. Howell, chairman of J.C. Penney Company, speaking at a recent NRMA convention said, "The old marketing methodology of consumer demographics will give way to psychographics. . . ." A quick trip to the dictionary revealed: "**psychographics**, the use of demographics to determine the attitudes and tastes of a particular segment of a population, as in marketing studies." In other words, more precise ways of slicing the various segments of the market. According to Howell, "The emergence of a multitude of lifestyle options and leisure time opportunities has created a marketplace with an increased number of segments." Thus, it is now urgent that you learn more about how your customers conduct their lives and on what they spend their money.

Until recently, most psychographic studies were conducted for the benefit of private business (unlike demographics collected by the Census Bureau and outfits such as Arbitron), and so much of the information is not available. However, a 1986 *Business Horizons* article fuses the results of their own study with some of that proprietary information. The magazine identifies seven distinct shopper types: inactive, active, service, traditional, dedicated-fringe, price, and transitional.

Bear in mind that these definitions are additional–not better–ways of examining your potential customers (much like cross-slicing orange segments). Here, then, is a summary of what BH found:

Inactive shoppers, making up about 15 percent of the total, are for the most part older consumers with limited enthusiasm for shopping. Their main concern is finding less complicated places to shop.

Active shoppers (12.8 percent of the total) shop more to express their lifestyles than to find bargains. They are middle-class, seeking moderately priced merchandise that looks more expensive.

Service shoppers (10 percent of the whole) demand a high level of service and quickly become impatient if kept waiting. While they are demanding, service shoppers represent a profitable market segment because they will pay higher prices rather than spend time looking elsewhere. They are usually loyal.

Traditional shoppers make up slightly more than 14 percent of the total and are big on outdoor activities. They are do-it-yourselfers, too, but are not fond of shopping. Apparently their modest upbringing makes them uncomfortable when spending money.

Dedicated fringe shoppers (8.8 percent) also like to do things themselves but feel almost compelled to be different. They exhibit limited brand and store loyalty, and go to a lot of trouble to learn about products on their own.

As the label implies, price shoppers (10.4 percent) are willing to search for bargains. They rely heavily on all forms of advertising to help them locate the best prices.

Transitional shoppers (just under 7 percent), on the other hand, don't shop around for low prices. They seem to be testing their own tastes and competence and are likely to be attracted by advertising campaigns that help them deal with their careers and social roles.

Another study, reported in the *Journal of Small Business Management* in 1986, revealed how most families feel about Sunday sales. It seems that many view shopping as good Sunday recreation. But small clothing stores were shown to be the least likely to open on Sunday, even though of all store types surveyed, they generated the largest percentage of their profits from Sunday sales.

Don Shapiro, president of First Concepts Development Corporation of Los Angeles, is a marketing consultant and educator. He says it's important for apparel store owners to be aware that each lifestyle has its own dress code. Of course, all teenage girls want clothing for young people. "That's kind of basic," he says. "But age alone will not tell you what their preferences and tastes are." He notes also that two business people with similar incomes, families, and single-family dwellings will buy totally different kinds of cars. Why? Their values, lifestyles, temperament, underlying preferences, and feelings are what guide people when they make choices as large as picking out a car or as small as buying pantyhose.

"If your idea of an apparel store is sophisticated, classy, upscale--a Fifth Avenue type," says Shapiro, "you'll be in for hard times if you locate it at the beach in Los Angeles. The age range may be the 20 to 30 you visualize, but the lifestyle will be wrong for your store."

Consider beach dwellers between 25 and 35, for example. A study of their lifestyle would reveal that their code of dress is recognizable. But not all women in that age bracket would be interested in the beach dweller's type of dress, only those who wanted to belong. Then they'd wear the clothing to proclaim to the world, "I enjoy the beach dwellers' lifestyle." You'll see the same phenomenon on the Sunset Strip in L.A. "If you want to belong to the crowd on the Strip," says Shapiro, "then you're going to dress rock 'n' roll." He notes that the music industry based in that part of Los Angeles has become a culture with its own style of dress and other values.

If you're part of a financial institution in the downtown section of any major city, Shapiro says, you would want to dress in a certain way, classic but interesting. Your clothing would show that you are successful in that environment. Psychographic studies done for the 1987 hit movie *Wall Street* revealed that big time corporate raiders have their own special image. If you want to seem to really belong--to be a power player--on "The Street," you'll wear suspenders. No amount of normal demographic study would lead you to that information. Only a study of the symbols a group of people with similar tastes and values have adopted to define themselves (in other words, psychographics) will uncover facts of that type.

Shapiro believes apparel is one of the most important symbols defining various groups. As an example, he points to women who are actively involved in fitness and exercise. In order not to feel "out of it" when they go to the gym, they must be wearing a certain kind of outfit. They must have certain leotards with stripes this way or that. Whenever they wear that outfit, they are looking for recognition as part of the group. If you were to interview ten of these women, you'd find some work and some don't, some own homes while others rent, but you'd find common psychological characteristics that bring them together. Successful marketers of exercise wear spend a lot of time in gyms, observing lifestyle trends.

"I advise all retailers," says Shapiro, "to listen to their customers, observe them, stay close to them. That's how you'll learn about their lifestyles, their tastes, and how their lives are changing." He suggests that many businesses just go on doing what they started out doing, basically never changing merchandise or methods that have been successful in the past. But customers are changing, aging, growing richer or poorer, taking on different values and jobs.

"My main message to retailers," says Shapiro, "is to find ways to stay close to your customers." He and other experts agree you don't have to spend a lot of money on expensive studies. Make it a point–even if you have a lot of people working for you–to get on the floor every single day. Talk to your customers to find out what's happening in their lives. Shop your competition, talk to as many of your suppliers as possible to let them tell you what's happening. Make it a point to sit down with your employees for a few minutes every day to see what customers have shared while they were being helped. Employees must know they should be alert for signs of change. Often they don't pay any attention to what the customer is telling them because they think no one higher up is interested.

Another thing you can do very inexpensively is put together your own little survey. Ask your customers what other stores they shop, what you can do to make their shopping more enjoyable, what they view as things you do right and wrong. You may want to have a drawing each month of all completed questionnaires. The winner gets a free dress, perhaps.

You might decide to stage a contest. Ask each customer to create an outfit from separates and accessories, not necessarily ones from your store. On a specified date have a fashion show of these outfits. A really terrific prize–a $250 gift certificate, say–goes to the designer of the most creative and original costume. You study all the entries to pick up on new trends or items that are missing from your shop. You'll be surprised at how much you'll learn about your customers and their tastes from such a promotion.

Solicit taste, preference, and lifestyle information from your customers constantly and use that knowledge to serve them. For example, call the client who is partial to red when a striking red dress arrives in the store. Train your staff to look for the individual likes and dislikes of your customers. Teach salespeople to learn, without seeming to pry, what kind of work the client does and in what kind of surroundings. You can develop your own psychographics file and keep it up to date as your customers' lives change.

Psychographic research has provided business planners with detailed information about why certain people buy their products. Convenient location and low prices are no longer good incentives. You must recognize lifestyles of women in your trading area, then find ways to appeal to their tastes and values.

Chapter Thirty-one:
DEALING WITH THE
IMPOSSIBLE CUSTOMER

"The customer may not always be right, but she's always the customer," reminds Roy Chitwood, president of Max Sacks, International, an employee training and consulting firm in Los Angeles. Since that ancient adage remains as true today as it was the first time it was uttered, and since without customers you'd be without a job, one of your main tasks is to work hard at being the kind of salesperson you like to have wait on you when *you* go shopping. And it's not always easy.

Arthur Schopenhauer has said, however, "To overcome difficulty is to experience the full delight of existence." It may be asking too much to expect you to regard cantankerous customers as a "delight," but if you regard them as a challenge you're on your way to coping with them successfully.

Roy Chitwood suggests four sound strategies for you to use when dealing with a customer who's in a bad mood. 1) Be receptive to what the customer is saying, no matter whether she's right, wrong, or indifferent. It doesn't really matter; she has a right to be heard. 2) Show genuine concern. By what you say to her and by your body and facial language let her know that you really care that she's unhappy about the dress that doesn't fit or the blouse with its hem unstitched. 3) Be a good listener. Don't let your thoughts wander while the customer lets off steam. Your eyes will reveal that you are no longer paying close attention to her problem. 4) Make sure you empathize with the customer. She must be convinced there's some basis for her complaint or she wouldn't have gone to the trouble to return the deficient item or taken the time to register a complaint. Be an active listener.

Typically, when an angry customer storms into a store, the salesperson who gets stuck with her *reacts*, instead of *responding*. There's a big difference. When the customer says, "This is wrong," you're reacting when you say, "No, it's not wrong." And often salespeople seem to take a special delight in proving how stupid customers are. Don't let that be the attitude you convey to a person whose goodwill is so essential to your own well being.

You should always respond to the customer by expressing concern, understanding, empathy, warmth. When you show no empathy or concern for the customer, what should be a minor situation develops into a major, serious problem because of your apparent indifference. According to Chitwood, every salesperson's challenge when she is confronted with a disagreeable or unreasonable customer is to turn that customer around. If you respond--not react--to her, you'll defuse her anger and placate her very quickly and probably turn her into a customer who will ask for you every time she enters the store.

Al Johnson, a teacher of Dale Carnegie courses in Los Angeles, agrees with Chitwood saying, "I would add only two pieces of advice. Treat the customer very respectfully and don't take her complaints personally." Whether she's right or wrong, she has a right to be treated with courtesy and deference and you aren't belittling yourself when you give it to her.

Penny Madden of Stuart Atkins, Inc., a human resources technology organization, says people are oriented to different styles of behavior and, hence, really speak different languages. "You must be sensitive to the customer's needs," she says, "trying to feel what they need, not what they say." Madden says her firm tries to help salespeople recognize phrases that reveal which behavior style is the customer's. You may want to observe the people around you, your friends as well as customers, to see if you can discover whether they are oriented toward harmony, excellence, action, or reason. Madden says her firm teaches salespeople how to deal with customers who are oriented in each of these directions. But even without formal instruction, you can--if you listen carefully--decide what is really motivating the complaining customer before you.

Don't leap to react to whatever the customer says or does that makes you label her "disagreeable." Try to figure out what it is she's really saying. When she shouts, for example, "You never have anything I like," she may really be saying, "I hate the way I look." If her complaint goes something like, "You don't ever have enough clerks to wait on people," she may really be saying, "I need my ego boosted today. Can't somebody take a little extra time with me?"

Perhaps you and another salesperson could try some role-playing. Take turns being the customer who makes your lives difficult. See if you can work out ways to show that you are concerned about the customer's unhappiness, that you are really listening to her complaint. It may be you'll come up with your own methods that will be just as helpful as these proposed by the experts.

In any event, when you truly hear what she's saying and remember how you felt when you had to take a problem to a clerk who lacked understanding, you're on your way to dealing most effectively with problem customers.

SECTION VII: PLANNING

Chapter Thirty-two:
PLANNING FOR
A NEW SEASON

For your store to be a success, you must have in stock the merchandise your customers want when they want to buy it. Attaining that deceptively simple-sounding goal requires that you work constantly to determine exactly what it is they want and plan to have it in stock.

Of course, your sales history will show what has sold well in the past, but to avoid missed sales you might develop a want slip that you fill out each time a customer asks for an item you don't carry. Perhaps you're missing some items that should be basic to your stock. Want slips and talks with customers will reveal if that's the case. Trade publications, too, can be a help in deciding what may be the next season's big sellers, since such publications often point out what items will be heavily advertised in coming months. Suppliers may be able to reveal what trends are getting started across the country, while comparison shopping will let you know what's moving well at stores in your neighborhood.

The data you gathered about your customers when you decided to set up shop (see chapter one) will be helpful to you also, when you decide what merchandise to stock in coming months. For your business success depends on your understanding your customers and providing them with products or services they cannot get from your competition. Imagination and foresight must be part of your planning, too, along with what you learn from your own store experience (that is, what items sold well in the past, which ones were dogs). Did you overbuy in some areas, buy too little in others? Proper planning is the key to avoiding these and other pitfalls of small store operation.

All of this knowledge will come into play when you make your merchandise plans, timetables of merchandising objectives to be reached during specified periods (usually six-month spans). The first includes spring (February, March, April) and summer (May, June, July) seasons. It should be finalized in the previous August to allow time for early buying of imports and other merchandise with long lead times. The second half-year plan covers August, September, October (fall), and November, December, and January (winter), and should be in place the preceding February.

This schedule is called a merchandise plan, but it's really a plan of action for the period. Your financial budget will have to be developed before you know how much you'll have to spend for merchandise. Your advertising schedule will need to be sketched at this time, too, to include that expense in the budget and to take advantage of suppliers' cooperative advertising whenever possible. Salaries, holidays, promotions . . . all must be woven into the fabric of a good plan.

One of the first important factors you must consider when you start to formulate a new seasonal plan is estimated net sales, that is, how much in dollars you can realistically aim for, based on your past experience and good judgment. Also influencing this calculation will be business conditions, competition, inflation, and any promotions you plan for the period.

Some retailers routinely plan for a five- or ten-percent increase in sales each year, but local economic conditions could make such a forecast futile. If one or more of the largest employers in your area has recently laid off most of its help, for example, you'll be wanting to think about down-sizing your operation until new industry takes up the slack. Or perhaps some new firms have come into your trading area, bringing well-paid employees with them. In that happy case, you might want to consider a greater increase in your sales projection or even an upgrade of your merchandise.

Critical to this plan is inventory records from previous years. How well did you do during this period a year ago? What stock items that were once big sellers are no longer moving? Which ones are you having trouble keeping in stock? What holidays fall during this period? Did last year's promotions succeed? Perhaps you'll want to plan more, fewer, different ones for this year. Now, when you're planning for next year, is the time to make such decisions. Markdowns and discounts must be part of your plan, too, for such factors affect the value of your inventory and next year's plan.

For each six-month period, you detail when you will next visit a market to study what's available for the coming season, when you'll place your orders, and when you must have delivery. The most carefully constructed plan cannot work if merchandise isn't on the shelves when you need it. Thus, you must include in your plan details of the merchandise you'll need each month (or season) and when it must be ordered.

Retailers look at the calendar date for the beginning of a new season as the merchandise date for the end of the old one. For example, March 21–from a merchandising point of view--is the end of spring, while June 21 is the end of summer and December 21 the end of winter. The period following the calendar date for the beginning of a new season is used by many retailers to sell closeouts, markdowns, off-price purchases and distress merchandise. Your spring reduced-price sale, for example, should be scheduled to start around March 21, when your summer merchandise has begun to arrive and you want to lure shoppers in to see it.

The amount of stock you'll order will depend on the amount of money you plan to spend to replenish stock sold. To arrive at this figure you consider planned sales and reductions, based on the previous year's activity, and factor in how much stock you have left over from previous periods.

When you place orders you must decide when to introduce new merchandise, when to reorder it, when to mark it down and, finally, when it should be removed from stock. Merchandise comes and goes like the tides; there should never be a time when something isn't happening to your inventory.

Calculating the quantities to buy during any given period is one of the most important aspects of merchandise planning. According to some experts, overbuying is the number one problem among retailers and one of the major factors leading to the first-year failure of 40 percent of all new stores. Even if you survive that critical first year, you can still run into trouble if you don't calculate accurately the quantities you need to purchase.

Planning purchases, then, is important. You arrive at the dollar amount by adding planned sales, planned reductions, and planned ending inventory for the period and subtracting the planned beginning inventory for the period. During any period, the dollar amount you have planned to spend less the amount you have already spent, or committed to spend, equals your open-to-buy. That's the amount you can use to replenish stocks during the period. Since each planning period has its own planned purchases, open-to-buy cannot be carried from one period to the next. If you chronically find you need to reorder too often, then you'll want to consider adjusting purchases in your six-month plan. Merchandise plans shouldn't be engraved in stone, however, but kept flexible so you can adapt to sudden changes in the retail weather.

Exercise inventory control, keep up with the changing tastes of your customers, read trade journals as well as consumer and business publications, talk to your customers and salespeople. In other words, keep a moistened finger raised so you'll always know which way the retailing wind is blowing. Then making a workable six-month merchandise plan will be a tough job, not an impossible one.

Chapter Thirty-three:
CREATING A
GOOD PLAN

As a general rule, your customers don't think of your store as a good place to buy a specific item. It's likely they look on it as the place to find a good assortment of merchandise they like within a price range that suits their budgets. Your biggest challenge as a retailer, therefore, is creating a mix that will successfully satisfy those expectations.

Once you've determined who your customers are, and thus what they expect from you, you draw up your model stock list, an outline of your inventory in terms of general characteristics. Past sales records will reveal your customers' tastes in fabrics, colors, and particular styles. Keeping a running check on these factors enables you to fill out your seasonal outline. Will it be mostly separates to mix and match, dresses, suits, or a mix? Sales experience helps you decide. Each class of merchandise will be identified by color, fabric type, and price line, but not by specific style numbers. After-five dresses in blue silk that sell for $79.95 might be an entry in your model, but your good fashion sense and what's popular for the season ahead will determine exactly how that dress will be styled.

Since there is always a certain amount of fill-in merchandise that must be ordered as a season progresses, a cardinal maxim of sound merchandising is to maintain at least some open-to-buy at all times. New goods arriving throughout the season will keep your customers' interest alive and enable you to take advantage of special concessions from your suppliers.

The secret to making a model stock plan and subsequent fill-ins work lies in coordinating styles and colors across all classifications. Consider, for example, a woman who always appears well dressed, yet doesn't spend a fortune on her clothes. She starts with a sound basic wardrobe--dresses, blouses, pants, jackets-- in styles and colors that all coordinate. She'll add new garments and accessories according to a plan, not by whim of the moment. While she may inject excitement into her wardrobe with a dress or suit that departs from her basic plan, everything else combines harmoniously to giver her a huge array of outfits.

Your merchandise assortment should be like the contents of that woman's closet: almost everything planned to coordinate with everything else. You'll select a variety of colors that complement each other, for example, and stylings that don't clash. If nautical is the look of the season, you'll order a lot of navy and white in pants, skirts, and jackets, all designed to go together. Accessories can be stocked in bold contrasts, as well as the basic colors, as long as they are suitable for the entire collection. Don't make the mistake of ordering skirts with ruffled flounces just because they're attractive and are offered at a good price. Stick to the theme and color scheme with which you started the season, until it's time for a whole new plan.

You probably won't want to order identical models to fill in–even if they are available–but you will want your mid-season arrivals to be compatible with both the color assortment and styling you started with. Scarves, belts, handbags, all accessories should be ordered and reordered within the limits of the seasonal theme.

Planned markdowns and mid-season promotions will help you move each season's stock so that you face the next buying period with just enough leftovers to have merchandise for your semiannual sales.

According to William Davidson, David Sweeney, and Ronald Stampfl in their excellent handbook *Retailing Management,* "One of the most common causes for an unbalanced inventory is the attempt to offer too great a variety of separate merchandise lines. . . ." You can maximize your profits and please your customers best by devising a coordinated plan of a fairly limited number of items. Then, if you should be out of a specific garment a customer requests, it will be easier to offer a substitute that will fill her needs equally well. It will be easier, too, to sell her additional items because she'll quickly see how they will fit in her overall wardrobe plan.

Think of yours as a store that creates a coordinated "look" for your customers, not one that sells individual garments. It will make a surprising improvement in your profit picture.

SECTION VIII:
YOUR EMPLOYEES

Chapter Thirty-four:
GOOD HELP--SCARCER THAN DIAMONDS?

Small retail businesses are the main entry into the world of work for many people, accounting for almost two-thirds of the "first jobs" available to young people. In 1985 nearly 17.4 million workers, about one out of every six nonagriculture wage earners, were employed in the retail trades, up by more than five million since 1970. And the trend continues, with most of the increase attributed to the sharp expansion in eating and drinking places and food stores. You don't have to be a demographics expert to realize that if the food service trades are expanding greedily and gobbling up what few work applicants there are, they are leaving fewer employees available for your business.

Historically the retail trade work force has differed in many respects from the general work force. For example, the industry has employed a disproportionately large share of part-time workers, women, and young persons. This profile has changed little in the last 15 years, but there have been some important changes within these groups. Much of the employment growth in retail trade has been in part-time jobs, with more than one in three of 1985's retail crew working part-time. No other industry had such a large proportion of its work force putting in fewer than 35 hours each week.

Part-time employment is so prevalent in retail trade because employers have found it an efficient way to meet the needs of consumers who nowadays shop around the clock and all week long. Consumer demand for some products varies by season, month of the year, and--in some cases--from hour to hour. To meet this fluctuating tide of demand, retailers must stay open longer hours and forget about weekend closings.

Many workers, students and mothers in particular, have a need for part-time jobs. In 1985, two-thirds of the retail part-time work force were women. For many women, part-time work allows them to help out the family budget and still be at home with the kids much of the time. Most young people who want part-time jobs are students.

Women accounted for more than half of all employees in retail trade in 1985, up just under two-thirds from the 1970 figure. This increase keeps pace with the growth of the number of women in the general work force.

Teenagers, on the other hand, accounted for one out of every five workers in retail trade in 1985, and more than half of all employed teens worked in retail trade.

With the aging of the baby boomers, fewer young people are entering the work force each year, in spite of the growing demand for the kind of service they usually render. To attract help, employers must offer well above the minimum wage. One economist says, "People aren't willing to work for even $5 an hour." That fact leaves a surplus of jobs that cannot be filled, even though national unemployment remains relatively high. According to an article in *Dun's Business Month*, by the early part of this decade, when most members of the baby boom will have moved on to better-paying, more challenging careers, there will be even more competition for the shrinking pool of workers. Consequently, employers will have to pay still more money for lower-quality employees.

Most retail store jobs are easy to learn and newly hired employees who have basic reading and writing skills can readily be trained by working alongside older hands. But young people with adequate literacy skills looking for work in the low-paying retail trade are growing increasingly rare.

Your need is for applicants who like to work with people and have enough innate tact to deal with difficult customers. A neat appearance, pleasant personality, and the ability to speak English clearly are other desired attributes. But employees with even such a limited range of skills and no experience can be costly. In 1984, the median wage for full-time apparel salespeople was about $5.30 per hour. Small wonder that annual turnover in the retail trades is usually about one million jobs vacated and refilled. Even part-time workers see themselves as needing more than the $185 a week or so, before taxes, they can earn working for an apparel store.

If your store is in a suburban area or in a city with inadequate public transportation, your staffing problems may grow still more severe. Few employees new to the work force can afford to buy and maintain cars. Older people--Social Security recipients who are limited in how much they can earn without forfeiting benefits--might seem to be an attractive solution, but many say they feel demeaned to be earning the same wages as "whippersnappers fresh out of school."

The outlook for small business labor is grim, with small retail stores having the dimmest future. Small business owners have cited not only changes in demographics of the work force, but also increased international competition, alarming illiteracy rates, and inadequate business education as factors that leave them wondering where they will find employees in the years ahead.

Chapter Thirty-five:
EMPLOYEES--YOUR
MOST VALUABLE ASSET

There's more to attracting and keeping good help than just figuring out how much to pay them. Of course, you must offer a fair wage to attract loyal, enthusiastic employees who will want to stay with you for many years. To define such a pay scale you'll want to take into consideration what percentage of your sales an employee generates, how much responsibility she is asked to bear, the complexity of her duties, and what special talents she contributes to the success of your business. Does she, for example, see to window and store displays? Does she write advertising copy, keep your perpetual inventory, or supervise other employees in your absence? Does she do ordering sometimes, or go comparison shopping on her day off? Any of these extra duties--extra in the sense of being above and beyond selling--call for extra compensation.

But how can you know how much each of these contributions is worth? And to what salary base will you add their value? Talk to someone at your chamber of commerce to find out the average pay rate for salespeople in your community. It is sure to have such information or be able to tell you where to find it. Read the want ads to learn how much full-time window display artists, copywriters, and so on make. Then calculate what fraction of the appropriate salary you'll want to add to the base rate of, say, a salesperson who spends two hours each week creating ad copy.

Some businesses make a practice of comparing notes with competitors in the area. One insurance supervisor, for example, says her company periodically calls the personnel departments of all nearby insurance offices to learn how much they are paying clerks, transcribers, and so on. You can poll the owners of retail stores in your mall or neighborhood to learn if the salary and commission you offer are competitive. But how can you make sure that some of the bright, eager young people in your area will seriously consider entering the retail industry?

Since the retail trades aren't noted for making millionaires out of paupers, you will have to offer rewards other than financial to attract and hold the best help. "The problem with most retail operations," says Bruce W. Barren, CEO of EMCO Financial Limited of Los Angeles, "is that they don't put a lot of energy into training the unqualified person they hire." Barren and his firm are noted for the quality of their financial advice and for having saved hundreds of foundering retailers from failure. He says most retailers look on job applicants as people who are just trying to fill their time and so can be had for $5.00 an hour or so. "Meantime," Barren adds, "they don't build employee loyalty."

According to Barren, managers have to pay attention to their employees. "Watch how they make a sale," he recommends, adding that you should explain that you're not there to criticize how the employee makes the sale, but to give constructive input. Barren notes that he tries to start with employees who are a little better than average. "Once I've hired them," he says, "I pay attention to them, try to graduate them up the pay scale through training." Most salespeople aren't trained to make multiple sales, he notes, and don't know how to turn a negative customer into a friend. An employee who has learned to deal with difficult customers is eminently more valuable than one who hasn't, Barren suggests.

"Treat your people as assets," he says, "your most important assets. Pay more attention to them. They are what trigger sales." He adds that advertising simply brings shoppers into the store; people make the sales but ads are given credit. Barren recommends that you learn the effective closing rate of your salespeople. Count the number of people who visit your store in response to a specific ad, then count how many of them actually buy something during that visit. That's the effective rate of your sales force. Praise them if it's high; train them better if it's low.

Look on your employees as long-term investments, Barren suggests. Give them the credit when business picks up or a promotion is unusually successful. Thank them for coming in early or staying late to help unpack a shipment. Give your people reasons to take pride in the sales they make; give them a reason to want to make more sales by praising them in front of associates. Encourage them to develop team spirit, to help each other with sales because they want your store to succeed. Install a suggestion box and use it. Make your employees aware that you consider their ideas important and acknowledge each suggestion. Act on the better ones, the ones that fit into your overall program.

Recognize that each employee has a life away from work. Allow them to work flexible hours, if possible; be understanding about family problems. But most importantly, let your employees know that the retailing industry can be rewarding. Let them have pride in their work--your store--and train them so that when they leave you they'll be able to command respect and good money anywhere. It's a safe bet, however, that it will take a lot of enticements to convince them to try their luck elsewhere.

Chapter Thirty-six:
MOTIVATION--MAKE
WORKERS OUT OF
SHIRKERS

It's not uncommon these days to hear business owners say one of their biggest problems is getting their employees to work. "They're lazy," many managers say, "and aren't committed to the company."

Psychiatrists and other people experts dispute the idea that employees don't want to work. In fact, some of the experts say, it's the nature of the human to want to be effective. Workers who seem to be lazy and lack motivation have probably had experiences that alienated them from work.

Besides wanting to feel effective, people also want to feel involved and cared about by other people, according to Edward L. Deci, professor of psychology at the University of Rochester and a specialist in human motivation. Employers should structure workplaces that nurture motivation, where people feel important when they're doing their jobs, Deci says.

What is motivation, anyway? Most experts agree that it's excitement about work. And when employees (as well as owners and managers) feel excited about their work, there is a good possibility that high achievement will follow. But you don't motivate your employees by hanging a sign on the wall that says, "Be Motivated Today." It's a way of life, a basic tenet of business. Creating the right climate is what keeps employees motivated. Something as simple, for example, as fresh flowers in your store every day may keep employee enthusiasm high.

One motivation tactic that some companies use is tuition repayment to help an employee advance. Perhaps you can't afford to pay even for night classes for your promising employees. According to a recent item in *Inc.*, they'll probably be equally motivated by a trick used by Davis, Hays & Co., a public relations firm in Hackensack, New Jersey: book reports.

Once a month an employee of the PR company talks about a book he or she has read. "We don't assign the book," says Alison Davis. "It just has to be related somehow to our business." She explains that the employee makes an old-fashioned book report, telling what the book was about, what was interesting, and what the reader learned that would help the company.

The company pays for the books, employees can read them on company time (when business is slow, of course), and the book reports are given during working hours. It's a training device for the entire staff.

Profit sharing and good health care insurance are motivators. So are a smoking policy that respects the needs of smokers as well as nonsmokers, a dress code that makes employees proud of the entire staff, and a firm stand on keeping drugs out of the workplace.

There's no test to measure exactly how much such policies will improve employee motivation--and, hence, efficiency--but it's a sure thing they'll build self-esteem. According to an employer in Lincolnshire, Illinois, "We want people to be as good as they're capable of being." He adds, "It's not so much that people who feel good about themselves do a better job; it's that people who do a better job feel good about themselves." And that, according to this employer, is a cornerstone of motivation.

Robert Grandford Wright, a professor of organization theory at Pepperdine University in Malibu, California, says the starting point in keeping a motivated staff is hiring only motivated people. That is, hiring people who feel good about themselves, who are interested in doing a good job, have integrity, initiative, intelligence, and communication skills. Then the manager's challenge, according to Wright, is to nurture that motivation, no simple task.

In the past, bosses did a lot of yelling, made their employees afraid they might lose their jobs, and the work got done. Today's workers, however, are a lot more sophisticated, more educated. They want to participate in decisions, to understand goals, and to help decide how these goals should be reached. Modern managers must be leaders, not shouting bosses.

Leaders have a clear vision of where their businesses are going and help their employees define their own goals. At a printing firm in Houston, for example, employees set new goals for themselves each quarter and at least one of the goals must be purely personal. Employees define their own goals and set up steps for achieving them. Their progress is reviewed periodically. It's how that company shows its concern for employees' success both on and off the job without seeming to be "sticking its nose into private affairs."

Leaders who motivate exude energy, projecting optimism and confidence. Employees will catch the mood. If you make it a point to develop your skills of writing, speaking, and--especially--listening, your workers will keep you clued in on how their morale is faring.

Another element in motivating your employees is being sure that they are thoroughly trained. "The problem with most retail operations," says Bruce W. Barren, CEO of EMCO Financial Limited of Los Angeles, "is that they don't put a lot of energy into training the people they hire." It isn't fair to just put a new employee on the sales floor and let her sink or swim. Take the time to teach her how to make multiple sales, how to turn negative customers into friends. Then, perhaps, hand the new employee over to an experienced one who will be her buddy until she feels confident about her own skills. The buddy answers questions, makes introductions, shows the new employee the ropes, helps her correct errors without making her feel stupid.

Motivating your employees is hard work requiring your constant efforts. Here are some tips from the country's best business owners and managers that you can copy.

Have a clear picture of your store and make sure employees know what it is. You might want to give each new employee a copy of your mission statement. Yours might be something as simple as "The goal of our store has always been to provide our customers with the best possible selection and fair prices along with the best service in the world." Make it obvious that you want customers to regard your store as the one place that can satisfy their apparel needs.

Give your employees praise. Say thank you for a good job. Write them notes of praise. Give out awards, trips if you can afford them, but even certificates will work. Praise them publicly whenever possible.

Recognize your employees' successes. Measure their productivity by dividing the number of sales they make by the number of customers they greet each day. (You'll probably want to weight sales for multiple items.) Keep a chart of the results where everyone can see it. Form a club of top performers and, perhaps, have a celebratory dinner every six months or so.

You may want to set up the chart so that employees receive even more honors for being on the roll for many months or years. Offer a special award, say a week's paid vacation or a trip to a local resort, for years of continuous top selling. Using the sales-to-opportunity ratio makes it possible for even part-time employees to compete with full-time old hands.

Communicate. Let your employees know how your business is doing and how they are doing. Keep them up to date on long-range plans. Listen closely, looking directly at them when they talk to you. And give them your full attention; don't be trying to solve some other problem while an employee is telling you something.

Involve your employees. Ask for their opinions and advice. If you're having difficulties, ask employees for helpful suggestions. Recognize all suggestions offered and be sure to credit the supplier of ideas that are put into action.

Back off. Don't stand at their shoulders during every sale and don't fussbudget about their activities when no customers are in the store. Let them decide what stock needs refolding or what displays need changing.

Be sensitive to each employee. Be sure they're assigned chores to keep them busy when they aren't selling. Nothing demotivates like boredom. But let the employees chose which tasks they'll do when. Let them own some responsibilities, tasks they'll perform when and as they choose. But make them realize they're important parts of the entire team.

Give rewards and incentives, but be careful that they don't come to be taken for granted. Give "spot rewards," too, say at the end of a big and successful sale. A voucher for dinner at a nice restaurant or tickets to a popular play or concert would be an appropriate reward for the long, hectic hours of a semiannual sale.

Be fair. Mary Kay Ash, of cosmetic party fame, says you should keep the Golden Rule in mind when dealing with your employees. Don't expect them to do something you wouldn't like to do. Set a good example by working just as hard as you expect them to.

Be calm, even in the face of disaster. Inspire confidence by keeping your cool and you'll find that your employees remain calm, too, and contribute to the solution of the problem.

Reprimand gently, not with shouting and table-thumping. Try to find out why the mistake was made and ask the employee for suggestions on how to keep it from happening again.

Most employees can handle such negative feedback, as long as they're working in an environment where they are told what they're doing right as well as what they're doing wrong and are made to feel good about themselves.

The key to the whole business of motivation is recognizing that people want to be effective in their work. Your job is to make it possible for them to succeed and then to let them know when they do.

Chapter Thirty-seven:
HOW TO TRAIN YOUR SALESPEOPLE

"Build a better salesperson and the world will beat a path to your door," says an ad in the *Los Angeles Times*. An effective sales force is composed of knowledgeable, interested people, the ad points out. People who want to hear from you, not talk at you. People who care more about your next question than their next commission. And people who won't give you a lot of guff--who won't say, "It's absolutely you, sweetie," unless of course it is.

It's obvious that the sentiments expressed in that ad embody the whole philosophy of retail selling, particularly of selling wearing apparel. But one big question clouds the issue: Who will help you train your salespeople to be knowledgeable, interested, and more aware that customers' satisfaction--or lack of it--directly affects their own paychecks? The answer to that question is elusive. "Salesman" training, that is, education for salesmen who call on industrial customers to sell windmills or widgets, is fairly plentiful. The Small Business Administration, for example, has some printed matter and seminars on that kind of selling, but little in retailing.

Management Aid number 5.001, titled "Checklist for Developing a Training Program" sounds promising until you read the "Summary" paragraph: "This Aid is designed to help owner-managers of small manufacturing firms set up a systematic program for training their employees." But before you discard the notion of spending 50 cents and a postage stamp to acquire this leaflet, consider another of its paragraphs. "Use this checklist as a guide. The experience of other companies in training can provide additional guides." The checklist then goes on to ask "What is the goal of the training?" and poses ten questions that could be very helpful to you if you should decide to devise your own training.

Subsequent sections ask "What does the employee need to learn? What type of training? What method of instruction? What audio-visual aids will you use? What physical facilities will you need? What about the timing? Who will be selected as instructor? Who should be selected (to receive the training)? What will the program cost? What checks or controls will you use?" Each section includes questions you must ask yourself when you're designing a program. Some of the questions don't fit the needs of retail stores, but some of them are most appropriate. If you have the time and energy to launch your own training program, you may want to order this pamphlet. Send fifty cents to SBA; Box 15434; Fort Worth, TX 76119. It will take about a month for the brochure to reach you.

Another SBA publication that will be peripherally helpful is a book you'll find at the Government Book store. It is Management Aid number 36 and is entitled *Training Salesmen to Serve Industrial Markets*. Chapters on the successful small firm are customer oriented. Other chapters that contain helpful advice are "The salesman's job," "Training your salesmen," and "Selling as a service." A representative of the SBA's SCORE (Service Corps of Retired Executives) suggests that material in the book, which is 85 pages long and costs about $2.50, could be adapted to retail training needs.

To set up a training program you'll need more than just a design; you'll want solid information, "how-to" to flesh out the skeleton you've shaped. Books should be the obvious answer to that part of the problem, but few authors have addressed the specific subject of selling at retail. Three who have are Annalee Gold and Elaine Stone and Jean A. Samples. Gold's book is helpful and specific. It is *How to Sell Fashion*, the second edition published in 1978 by Fairchild Publications of New York.

This volume includes such chapters as "How to increase effectiveness of salespeople," "What salespeople should know: techniques of selling," "Changing patterns in fashion merchandise, and "Customers list their pet peeves." You'll find this book both interesting and helpful as you plan how to train your salespeople.

Elaine Stone and Jean A. Samples are the authors of *Fashion Merchandising: An Introduction*. The fourth edition was published in 1985 by McGraw-Hill, Inc. The authors' acknowledgments include names of educators and experts at more than a dozen schools and industrial organizations such as Hinds Junior College in Raymond, Mississippi, the Fashion Institute of Technology in New York City, and the Fashion Institute of Design and Merchandising in Los Angeles. You might find some of the same people willing to help you out as you try to create a training program. The text of this book isn't nearly so explicitly helpful as the one mentioned above, but it does cover a great deal about the history and general aspects of selling fashion merchandise. And chapter seven, "What salespeople should know: techniques of selling," contains some good examples of selling situations. The chapter closes with a list of do's and don'ts that will repay almost any effort or cash you have to expend to find the book. Ask the librarian at any good-sized library for these volumes or others that may be available on the subject. It's a good bet you'll come up with something helpful.

If your home or store is near a university library, you may be able to consult back issues of *Magazine of Human Resources Development* and *Training and Development Journal*, two publications that address the problems of training sales help. Most consumer magazines don't take up issues involved in store owners' problems, so publications such as these are your best bet. Once again, ask your librarian to help you locate any journals that might offer helpful information.

Still another source of help you may locate through your library is computer software for training. Much of this material, too, is geared to the salesman who sells to industry, not to consumers. But you may discover helpful hints by reading reviews of the software published in computer magazines. (Tip: If your library subscribes to it, use the "Business Index" to locate magazine articles that can be helpful to you in many aspects of your business as well as in the area of training. Ask your librarian to show you how to use the Index. Mastering it will be time well spent.)

But the most valuable resource your library has, by far, is *The Audio Visual Market*, a directory of organizations involved in the production and distribution of videotapes. For the world of the future in training lies in tapes, movies if you will, that can be played again and again on VCRs at your store, home, or any facility you choose.

The directory has a section devoted to firms that deal with sales promotion and training programs. In that part of the book are listed scores of companies that produce training films and make them available for sale or rental to anyone interested. As a matter of fact, films that are responsible for the stellar salespeople mentioned in the opening paragraph of this chapter are produced by The Friedman Group, a Los Angeles firm that specializes in teaching the art of retail sales.

Harry Friedman, founder and president of the Friedman Group, has led National Retail Workshops since 1980. With a staff that includes an industrial psychologist, Friedman conducts workshops for salesclerks, often moving his classroom into their stores. In his seminars and workshops Friedman teaches how to open the sale, how to probe to determine the customer's wants and needs while you develop her trust in you. He also shows how to demonstrate the value of the merchandise, how to close the sale, handle objections, and a lot more.

Friedman also has a consulting division that works with private clients all around North America. "We have audio and video programs, too," says Friedman's assistant Fran Coleman, "both generic and specific areas. The apparel industry is one that needs us so badly we have not yet been able to do all we can." At the moment, Friedman is working with the National Retail Merchants' Association to develop sales training for apparel retailers.

"I train salespeople how to communicate with customers," says Friedman, who points out that his entire selling program is on tapes costing $600. That price includes workbooks and leader's guide plus 8 modules on videotape. "It's a great deal," says Friedman. It is also available on audiotape for $149, but, says Friedman, "The video is worth the price for added sales." He adds, "The future is in salespeople. It's where the additional profits are. It's time clothing merchants face up to this and start investing in professionalism. Merchandise is all alike; everybody's cutting prices, so all you have to offer [your customers] is better salespeople." Unfortunately, Friedman's films are available only for sale. But he suggests that a group of small retailers might cut individual costs by joining forces to put on a training seminar for their combined staffs. For details about tapes from the Friedman Group or for a free subscription to *On the Floor*, a quarterly publication full of helpful tips, call (800) 351-8040.

A tape production firm whose films are available on a rental basis is Excellence in Training (etc) in Des Moines, Iowa. Becky Erickson, a spokesperson for the firm, says you can call them collect at (515) 276-6569 if you're seeking information about their training tapes or lectures. They can do research for you, produce custom tapes, provide speakers, at a cost per production of about $2500 to $5000 or even more. Noncustom tapes, on the other hand, cost between $395 and $595. Says Erickson, "A guide for the leader of the training session and workbooks for all participants will cost under five dollars each," in addition to the cost of the tape. She, too, suggests purchasing the tape and clubbing together with other store owners in your area to put on a seminar. However, tapes can be rented for about $95 for a two-day rental to about $125 for five days. "The only other costs," says Erickson, "would be the workbooks and guide books, plus the fee for a trainer to conduct the program and rental for a site at which to hold it." It could be a very inexpensive way to train your help, she says.

Etc doesn't have a tape that addresses the problem of understanding the specific needs of career women in different fields and at different management levels. Indeed, Erickson doesn't know of any group that has addressed that topic for public use. You may have to seek help from one of the country's fashion institutes or similar schools.

On the other hand, Erickson says, "We have a video called 'Relationship Selling,' how to adapt your selling style to the customer." It looks into analyzing the personality of the customer and the preparation that's needed for each sale and how to start the necessary relationship that will make closing the sale possible.

It appears that finding the resources you'll need to help you train your salespeople can be a difficult task. But contact some or all of the sources mentioned here and you'll soon be on your way to creating the best sales staff in the world, or at least in your corner of it.

Chapter Thirty-eight:
SAY NO TO
EMPLOYEE THEFT

Employees have as many ways of stealing from you as you have employees. Indeed, employee theft is considered by many experts to be the main cause of stock shrinkage. Dr. David Cherrington, professor of organizational behavior at Brigham Young University, believes that as much as 60 percent of shrinkage can be blamed on employee theft. Mark Lipman, a private investigator who specializes in ferreting out employee theft, estimates that it costs American business up to $40 billion each year and accounts for between five and thirty percent of all business failures.

The growing shortage of good help is probably one of the major reasons for the increase in employee theft. Many employers are being forced to lower their standards and hire people they would have turned away just a few years ago. Additionally, to avoid possible legal complications, most firms no longer release information about former employees. When asked for references, personnel officials often will verify only dates of employment and salary ranges. If an employee was dismissed for stealing, the odds are good that a prospective employer won't be told about it.

Most experts in the field agree that it's impossible to eliminate employee theft entirely. You can, however, reduce the amount you lose. First, you'll want to foster a climate of honesty. Be scrupulously honest yourself in all matters, large and small. Talk about how much damage theft does to businesses like yours; make your employees realize shrinkage can cost them pay raises and benefits--maybe even their jobs. You may want to institute a program of bonuses for shrinkage reduction, even profit-sharing. Whatever programs you undertake in this regard, let your help know they have a stake in the action. Make it worth their while to stop employee theft.

Talk about your theft policy often, casually and in staff meetings. Broadcast the message that theft will not be tolerated. Give each new employee a handbook or written statement that clearly spells out the consequences of theft: instant dismissal. Enforce a tough antitheft policy at all levels and never make exceptions, no matter what excuse an employee pleads.

Let workers know that you care about them as well as your property. Be sensitive to employee morale. Be alert for disgruntled employees who complain about too much work or too little pay. Provide a system for airing such gripes and solving problems before they get too big. Get rid of employees who seem to have a grudge against you or other employees.

Make employees feel a part of the team. Solicit their suggestions on how to reduce shrinkage. Don't offer rewards for actual spying, but make it possible for them to tell you if they have suspicions about how losses occur.

Remove temptation by putting in place whatever controls you can manage. Divide responsibilities so the person who keeps your books doesn't also have charge of inventory. A setup such as that can make it too easy for that employee to pilfer without your being aware until it's too late.

Make sure employees know you are always checking, keeping a close eye on your assets. Don't just replace items sold; use control systems that monitor transactions against norms and analyze inventory flow. If too many of an item–particularly an expensive one–are removed from inventory, be sure legitimate sales and not pilferage account for the removal.

Invoices, shipping tickets, purchase orders, and credit slips should always be countersigned to ensure that phony sales and orders aren't being used to rip you off. Prenumbered sales receipts and invoices or cash register receipts will reduce the temptation for employees to pocket cash from sales.

Theft of costly items is fairly easy if you allow boxes to pile up in the stockroom. An employee can put a garment or two into boxes and set them outside the back door to pick up at the end of her shift, or have an accomplice collect at once. Have all boxes crushed before they are disposed of and keep back entrances locked, if fire laws permit.

Look into installing a system that audits each employee's transactions. Doing such a chore manually can be time-consuming, but computer programs are available to do the job. One such program is Stoploss, available through TMB Enterprises in Lynwood, Washington. That program stores cash-register activity and employee schedules. It analyzes stored cash-register data and employee schedules, flagging unusual transactions or ones that occur more often than expected. Flagged transactions are matched with the salesperson responsible. If one employee is often singled out, you may want to have a talk with that person. While this process sounds complex, it takes only a few minutes on the computer.

An even simpler means of deterring employee theft is to conduct regular and frequent inventory audits. You can do them yourself, but authorities recommend that you occasionally have an independent auditor take over. Be sure that these audits aren't done on a regular schedule, allowing a thief to cover her tracks just before an audit.

Your best means of preventing employee theft, however, is using great care when hiring. Don't invite the fox into the henhouse, so to speak. Dishonest employees are harder than ever to spot, since the courts have made polygraph tests illegal for screening applicants, but extra vigilance pays off.

Verify all references. Look up previous employers' phone numbers yourself to make sure you won't be calling a phony who will give you a glowing report. Check the credit ratings of applicants. According to the National Retail Merchants *Association (NRMA) in a handbook titled Apprehending and Prosecuting* Shoplifters and Dishonest Employees, credit agencies can legally furnish information about not only a person's credit history, but also general reputation, personal characteristics, or mode of living. You may even want to ask state and local police if a would-be employee has a criminal record.

Some store owners are turning to pencil and paper tests to give them an idea of the honesty of potential employees. Such testing has been found to weed out dishonest job applicants, identify reliable workers, and reduce employee theft, according to an article in a recent issue of *Chain Store Age Executive*.

The tests cost from about $7 to $15 for each candidate, depending on the number you buy. Moreover, many of the tests are designed so that you can score them yourself, sometimes with score analysis provided over the phone at no additional cost. Some can be scored and analyzed by your computer, too.

It usually takes about half an hour for an applicant to complete one of the tests, which typically consist of from about 60 to more than 100 multiple choice questions. An applicant's answers to test questions will reveal certain character traits, including opinions about dishonest acts committed by others. Some firms who produce the tests claim they can reduce employee theft by as much as 50 percent. Look in your Yellow Pages under "Test Publishers" to locate a supplier in your area.

Employee theft is a growing problem for retailers, but you can do a lot to reduce your losses. Just remember that a few hours spent on prevention will be far more effective than weeks of trying to work a cure.

Chapter Thirty-nine:
HELPING HANDS
ON REQUEST

Have you ever thought, I'd try that (a survey, statistical study, or whatever) if only I had an extra pair of hands? The extra hands you need to improve some aspect of your business may be available at the nearest university or community college. Most schools, depending on their size and curricula, offer some kinds of advice and assistance to local business people.

AT UCLA, for example, the Graduate School of Management offers an internship course that involves 70 to 80 hours of student fieldwork during a 10-week quarter. This course is designed to provide students with opportunities to apply what they've learned to real business situations. Assignment of an intern to a business depends on a written proposal that details the scope of the problem to be solved, the type of work expected of the student, and the assignment of a person in the firm to assume responsibility for the student.

Community colleges may not have such formally structured programs, but instructors in appropriate disciplines might be willing to ask for volunteers who wish to gain experience in their chosen fields. In both of these cases, the business owner would be expected to reimburse students for out-of-pocket expenses.

A third possible source of the added hands you need may be the placement bureau of your local institution of higher education. Many students, pressed for cash to meet expenses, are eager to take on jobs in their fields of study. You should be able to hire a management student, say, for a fraction of what the services of a full-fledged consultant would cost.

Free extended personal counseling is offered to small business owners through the cooperation of faculty and students of business schools with the Small Business Administration. For more information on this source of assistance, contact: Small Business Institute, Office of Management Counseling Services; Management Assistance, Small Business Administration; 1441 L Street, N.W.; Room 602-H; Washington, DC 20416.

Give your nearest college or university business school a call. It's a good bet you'll locate that extra pair of hands you need to solve your business problems.

Chapter Forty:
IS THERE A COLLEGE GRAD IN YOUR FUTURE?

Big retail chains are bidding for the services of business school and liberal arts grads in unprecedented numbers. How come? Such businesses need hundreds of bright, eager people to staff their stores. Graduates who haven't made a career choice are ideal recruits. And those who have chosen marketing as their field find stores standing in line to hire them. Terri Coons, lecturer in retail management at USC's School of Business, says there are many good reasons for that phenomenon. "College is a maturing process," she points out, "so that in itself makes these young people a better risk, no matter what their majors." She goes on, "Also, if they do take some retail classes in college, that prepares them with a better understanding of the terminology, the vocabulary. They know what to expect as far as the job goes, in the matter of pay and so on. They're not as much in the dark."

On the other hand, a study reported in a recent issue of the Los Angeles *Times* claims to have found "widespread complacency, poor planning and a lack of contact with the business world," in the nation's business schools. "While both corporate and academic leaders believe business schools are performing reasonably well at present, they are in danger of drifting casually toward the 21st century, without careful thought and strategic planning about the roles their graduates will play in the changing world of business," the study said. It faulted schools for teaching corporate long-term planning while doing little more, themselves, than planning for the next semester.

In spite of criticism directed at business schools, retailing executives view the possession of an M.B.A. in a very positive light. One large chain personnel director said, "We interview dozens of them each year and add a few to our staff each time. They have valuable skills."

Dr. Drully Blotnick, a psychologist and specialist in business matters, says apparel retailers have learned the value of education. "Industries . . . that depend too much on the 'creative' mystique would do well to pay attention to what's going on in retailing, where the smartest operators have learned how to mix show biz and the MBA approach most effectively."

Why, then, is turnover so high among retailers? Jordan Marsh, for example, loses a quarter of its recruits in the first year. Bloomingdale's loses 20 percent and Macy's about a third. In the big stores money isn't the issue, apparently, since many buyers earn a minimum of $30,000 yearly.

A recent article in *Forbes* lays some of the blame on long hours required of new hires. These young people are expected to work 12-hour days and many weekends, not quite the bankers' hours many of them expected.

Are these school-trained young people worth the greatly increased salaries they command? Coons says, "In the past few years retailers realized that they weren't getting the best graduates from colleges because their beginning salaries were too low. So most retailers have increased their entry-level salaries in order to attract more and better students."

What can graduates expect beyond long hours and fairly good pay? Coons says, "They're recognized as the future of the company." Even though they may be expected to perform menial tasks and be subjected to pressures from people in different parts of the business, they're in management training spots. Management is going to be looking to them to see how they're progressing. "Retailers recognize that these kids just out of college want challenges beyond just selling merchandise," says Coons. That expectation has been answered by most big retailers by giving the kids more responsibility. Two or three months after graduation, according to Coons, some of them will be managing departments that do $2 or $3 million plus in business. "It's a big responsibility and the kids won't get bored," she says.

Coons notes, and most small apparel store owners agree, that if you own a small store, chances are you're not going to be able to pay the $20,000-plus starting figures these kids are getting from the likes of Macy's and Nordstrom's. It's a fact, too, that most of the college grads won't consider part-time work that most stores like yours offer. "So maybe," she says, "you want to hand pick the cream of the crop from high school and if they stay with you for a year or so, send them to school yourself." She also suggests that you might want to hand-pick your trainees from the best of what trade schools have to offer. A lot of these kids aren't interested in going to work for big mega-companies, she thinks, and might welcome overtures from a smaller store where they can accomplish more, faster.

"Turnover and lack of loyalty are so high," though, she cautions, "that any training is chancy. Companies are screening more carefully, not just looking at grade point averages, but also considering personality traits. You know, what makes a good retailer?" She says you'll want to look for students who have the entrepreneur spirit, are creative, have analytical ability, and can keep multiple balls up in the air at the same time. They must have good command of English, too, and good communication skills.

Will small retailers like you be able to attract some of the promising young people from recent graduating classes? You'll have to find the few who will put job satisfaction ahead of the fast buck or choose eager and bright high school grads who show a lot of promise. It's a risky proposition, true, but you do stand a chance of developing a creative, helpful employee who will want to see your business grow as much as you do.

Chapter Forty-one:
MBO--A PHILOSOPHY,
NOT A REMEDY

Management by objectives (MBO) is a philosophy of management, not a magic potion for business ills. For decades management gurus and new-idea consultants have pushed one quick fix after another: quality circles, one-minute managers, corporate culture, and the rest. All these fads have been heralded as cures for such ailments as disappearing markets and low employee productivity; all have proved to be less than successful. But MBO, practiced skillfully, continues to be a sound technique for steering corporate craft through the shoals and reefs of an unpredictable business world.

To be successful an MBO system needs to answer two questions: "Where do I want to go?" (the answer to this question provides the objective), and "What pace should I set for myself?" (this answer gives you feedback on interim progress). It's not enough, however, for only top managers to be aware of corporate objectives; each subordinate level must share those objectives and have a stake in attaining them. "Instill shared goals throughout the corporation," says James E. Lee, chief executive officer of Gulf Oil. "Communicate these goals to all employees."

For example, if you decide to visit Aunt Minnie for your next vacation, you'd surely discuss with your spouse and children where you (and they) are going. Getting to Aunt Minnie's becomes a shared objective of your family. Since you leave it up to the family to plan the details of the 2,000-mile drive, their objective is to formulate a route. You wouldn't expect them to plan the trip without knowing its destination. But many managers fail to reveal their objectives to subordinates, while still expecting them to help attain corporate goals.

Management by objectives requires that goals be agreed upon before resources are released, effort expended. In this way, the effectiveness of the organization is enhanced, its activities focused, and the definition of individual success within the organization is made clear. MBO answers the question, "Are we doing the right things?" rather than "Are we doing things right?" It also spells out constraints under which operations will be conducted, constraints that might include laws, company policies, values of the founders. One example of such a constraint is Gerber's motto: "Babies are our business . . . our only business."

At the corporate level, objectives are defined based on resources, market position and opportunities, and managerial capabilities. At the operating level, corporate objectives are divided into departmental objectives, then strategies--the means by which to accomplish goals--are developed. Each level develops its own objectives, based on how that level of management perceives its share of corporate objectives. The next-higher level of management approves sublevel objectives, but does not determine the strategies for attaining them.

For example, you might define as one of your company's objectives "Decide whether to open another store in the new shopping mall across town." To reach that decision you need to know what stores are available, what equipping a new outlet will cost, how you will staff it, what kind of sales you can expect in the new location. You call on appropriate groups or individuals to do the necessary investigation. You don't tell each group *how* to accomplish its task, just *when* you need the information and how much money each group can spend. When you are given the reports about personnel, costs, stores available, and so on, your subordinates have attained their objectives and enabled you to reach yours. Even if you decide the new store's not a good idea right now, you've accomplished your objective, which was to reach a decision.

Managing by objectives, then, is defining and pursuing attainable objectives, deciding where you want your company to go in relation to where it is now. But objectives must be quantitative. Saying, "We want to develop a better cost control system," is not defining an objective. Neither is deciding "We need to improve our sales." However, you might decide conditions are right to go for a sales increase of ten percent in the next year. Such an improvement in business is measurable; it is clear; it is attainable. It is a legitimate objective.

To accomplish a measurable increase in sales will require the cooperation of at least the selling employees, advertising department, and buyers. Therefore, once you have formulated the objectives and attendant constraints (how much you'll spend on advertising, from whom you'll buy the larger number of garments, whether to hire additional salespeople or ask employees to work overtime, and so on), you'll want to meet with managers of the areas involved. You will reveal to them the goal of a ten percent increase in sales and ask them to develop departmental objectives to help you meet it. Once you have approved their objectives, managers are free to develop their own strategies for reaching them. But the operating departments must recognize that day-to-day actions and decisions are not isolated from one another. Even difficult problems must be solved in ways that will not hinder the attainment of objectives.

Management by objectives has proved so successful in part because it provides feedback about the specific task at hand. It shows you how you're doing so you can make adjustments without waiting for a year-end report to reveal that you didn't meet your goal. Since objectives below the corporate level should be based on a yearly plan, feedback from quarterly reviews will reveal how close you are to reaching your goals. If any department seems to be falling short, the manager can develop better strategies for the next period.

The secret to successful management by objectives is maintaining the proper balance between coordinated effort and the freedom of action necessary to allow each manager to develop fully within a flexible organization. The organization must depend on its managers at all levels to exercise the initiative and discretion necessary to make the organization thrive. Since managers formulate their own objectives and strategies, they know their ability and worth will be measured by how well they succeed at attaining those objectives. Thus, they aren't likely to become involved in empire building or office politics, but will focus their efforts and talents on reaching the goals they defined for themselves. It's a sound method of insuring that both your company and your employees will continue to grow and prosper.

SECTION IX:
SOLVING CASH PROBLEMS

Chapter Forty-two:
SOLVING A
CASH FLOW DILEMMA

So; you have a cash flow problem and don't know where to turn. Plenty of friends and authorities will be happy to advise you how to spot such a crisis in the making, but few are very helpful when it comes to working out of the problem once it has developed.

Such a difficulty arises when your accounts receivable climb substantially over what they were in the same reporting period during previous years. Reasons for the problem can be hard times, a poor job of collecting on your part, a too-liberal credit policy, or having had to dump merchandise that didn't move as you expected it to, thereby reducing the amount of cash flowing into your business.

There are some steps you can take to get out of this morass, but you don't want to end up digging a deeper pit. The most obvious solution would seem to be a short-term loan to tide you over until money starts pouring in a little more freely. Many banks, however, are reluctant to lend money under these circumstances. And loans always have the drawback of interest. If you do succeed in getting a loan, will you really be any better off paying back $1100 or more for every $1000 you manage to raise?

You may want to bill your outstanding accounts sooner and more often. If you have a great deal of money tied up in charge accounts, you may want to divide your customers into two cycles that you bill on the 15th and last day of each month. You'll spend more on all aspects of billing, but you should make cash flow in more smoothly.

Phillip Kavesh and Tom Gau, financial counselors of Torrance, California, suggest that you offer a discount of, say, two percent or so, to your charge cutomers who pay their bills within ten days. "Stand back and watch the cash flow in," says Gau.

Perhaps you're considering selling your accounts receivable to a factor. It's possible, of course, but only as a last resort. Factors usually demand a high discount on the accounts they buy. The same can be said for collection agencies. You could turn your late-paying accounts over to one of them for collection, but collectors often keep up to half of what they take in and you are almost certain to alienate the customers whose accounts you refer.

What about having a <u>big</u> sale and disposing of a large part of your inventory? Offer an extra discount for cash sales. But remember, you're probably just shifting purchases to the present and away from the next several months.

Or you may want to delay payment on accounts payable. In this event, of course, you lose possible discounts and may alienate the supplier you ask to wait for payment. You might even find yourself placed on a cash-only basis with some vendors.

Once you have solved the problem for the moment--by whatever means--you want to make sure it doesn't happen again. The first permanent step to take is to make sure your accounts are billed on time and collection is vigorously pursued. You don't want to find your business in a cash flow bind every other month or so. Perhaps you should look into acquiring an accounts receivable program tailored to your needs. Retail Merchandising Service Automation, Inc. (RMSA) offers a sophisticated system that automates all aspects of billing. If you or your financial advisor think you could ease some of your problems with such a system, call (800) 251-0231 for details or write to Accounts Receivables; 6600 Jurupa Avenue; Riverside, CA 92504.

You may even want to discontinue offering credit, although you could lose a number of customers by taking that route. The National Retail Merchants Association (NRMA) has found that offering credit literally means business these days. NRMA reports that stores with in-house charge accounts are averaging 24 percent more business than those who don't offer that service.

RMSA suggests that most cash flow problems can be averted by careful inventory management, making sure that merchandise flows in at the times specified in your orders. "From the standpoint of both cash flow and turnover, it is apparent that when new merchandise arrives within 30 days prior to the season, the store remains better prepared to manage its stock profitably." RMSA sells both electronic and manual systems for assuring that the flow of merchandise is such that you will always be selling from fresh stock, without an undue number of markdowns. Good inventory management is the key to success in this instance.

By all means, consider engaging the services of an accountant or financial advisor who will examine your entire business and make recommendations for other ways to stay out of cash flow trouble. Consider, too, the Small Business Administration and its SCORE program. A local office should be listed in your phone book, or call (202) 653-6279.

Chapter Forty-three:
CASHING IN
ON YOUR ASSETS

When you're always short of ready cash and find yourself setting some bills aside to "pay next month," or holding back on placing an order in time for your next big selling event, you don't have to be told you have cash flow problems. You're not alone. A common blunder committed by many small business operators is putting too much money into capital assets, leaving too little to meet day-to-day expenses and replenish inventories.

You can't sell from empty shelves, however; your continued success depends on having an adequate inventory. If you come up short in providing what your customers have grown to expect from you, you'll lose them and compound your cash flow problem with reduced sales.

What can you do? Fortunately, finding cash for your company merely takes some imagination and a hard look at assets you can quickly, and relatively painlessly, convert to cash. The right solution for you, of course, depends on your unique business and its problems. But some of the following tips for acquiring cash in a hurry are sure to help.

- If you own the building your business occupies, try to sell it and then get a long-term lease. Repair and upkeep costs may become a thing of the past, too, if you can negotiate for the new owner to take them on.

- If you have a month-to-month or even a single-year lease, try to negotiate a longer one at a better price. If the mall or area you're in has a high vacancy rate, the owner may be eager to accommodate you. Remember, though, that you'll have to buy out the lease if you should decide later to move to another location.

- Sell your fixtures (they're probably outdated, anyway) and lease more modern ones.

- Sell your rounders and racks and replace them with wall hangers that you build yourself. If you're not handy with tools, try to work out a trade agreement with a local carpenter.

● Sell the small-business computer you installed for billing and inventory control. Then sign up for a computer time-sharing service. Such firms generally have ready-made programs that will meet all your needs or can be easily--and inexpensively--adapted. Start-up costs are low and you'll be charged only for the time the computer is actually in use. Most metropolitan areas have several time-sharing vendors listed in their yellow pages.

● Get rid of any luxuries you've acquired. That means selling off the fancy desk and expensive rug in your office, eliminating extension phones and optional telephone services that you can do without. Keep monthly costs down, too, by exercising strict control on employees' phone calls.

● Lease any excess space you may have. Such a plan would work especially well if you let the space to a business that complements your own. A retailer of handbags (if you don't carry them) is one possibility, as is a hat seller.

● Lease your private office to an accountant or tax-preparer. Set up a little cubbyhole in a corner for your own desk space. (See chapter six). Rent out your basement, if you have one, for storage. Or, if local regulations permit, lease your roof space for an outdoor ad. Be creative in spotting areas you can rent without hindering your own activities.

● Sell off a portion of your inventory that isn't moving well. You might put on a "raising cash" sale or try to find a jobber that will take the entire lot off your hands. Consider taking on consignment an especially attractive new line you can't afford to buy right now.

● If your store looks shabby after all these changes, and you can't find the money for a decorator, fix it up yourself. A little paint will work wonders for your spirits and help boost sales. Ask if your local college has interior design students that might--for school credit and very little cash--give you some decorating tips.

These suggestions are only a beginning. Take a hard look at your assets, letting nothing escape your attention. Anything that isn't nailed down is a candidate for sale or trade for less-expensive models. When you've done all you can, you'll have a lean operation, the kind in which more cash flows in than out.

Chapter Forty-four:
HOW TO SAVE ON
FREIGHT CHARGES

No matter how small your business is, you can reduce the amount you must spend on freight bills. In fact, according to Dorothy Geiss, traffic manager of the Strauss Stores in Youngstown, Ohio, transportation is one of the few business costs that will vary in direct proportion to the amount of control exercised by the retailer. You or a qualified employee should take over the functions handled by the traffic manager of a large company: routing shipments, auditing freight charges, and handling damage and loss claims. In one recent year the May Company reduced its transportation costs by more than 12 percent by carefully monitoring freight charges. Can you effect similar changes in your operation? Probably.

These are the chores you'll need to take on for greatest possible savings: See that all merchandise you order is routed properly. Unless the vendor is paying shipping charges, you have a right to route the shipment. And charge vendors for any extra freight costs that arise because they didn't follow routing instructions.

Verify rates charged by freight carriers. You should check all freight bills for accuracy and then turn them over to an independent auditor. Commissions charged for auditing vary, although the usual fee is 50 percent of the amount of overcharges collected. In addition, good auditors often do more for you than just collect overcharges. They may know of better freight terms being received by other stores; frequently they can suggest ways to consolidate shipments; and they may discover erroneous freight classifications in use by vendors. Contact the National Retail Merchants Association for the names of companies in your area who perform freight bill audits.

You also want to be sure your buyer is equipped with comparative freight rates and transit times from different points of origin. The buyer should always bear in mind that a more costly mode of transport may be the most cost effective if it gets your merchandise to you much faster than the lower cost mode. Thus armed, the buyer may be in a position to negotiate better agreements with vendors. Control routing of all returns, too, and insist that the vendor pay return freight costs if a return is necessitated by some failure on the vendor's part.

Arrange for consolidation of small shipments. J.C. Penney managed to save almost 44 percent recently on a typical shipping charge from Boston to its store in Fresno, California, by consolidating shipments from several suppliers. In some areas retailers have formed cooperative associations to arrange just such small shipment consolidations. If you are a member of a retail merchants' group in your area, you may be able to participate in such an association. MSA Lamda, Inc., is a coast-to-coast nonprofit shipping association based in Los Angeles. While most of its 300 or so members are manufacturers, retailers are welcome to join for a $75 annual membership fee. Call (213) 265-3900 to learn if this organization can be helpful to you. You'll find other freight consolidators listed in the yellow pages of major cities.

Finally, trace and expedite overdue shipments and file promptly claims for merchandise lost or damaged in transit. The amount you save on freight charges may not be as large as those realized by Penney and May Company, but you can be sure you will save if you exercise strict control over your merchandise shipments. And if all these necessary chores seem to be beyond your expertise, look in the yellow pages for the name of a freight traffic consultant who will do most of them for you, probably for substantially less than the amount you'll save.

Chapter Forty-five:
HOW TO SAVE CASH
WHEN YOU TRAVEL

Wouldn't it be great if you were on an expense account when you go to market each season? You wouldn't have to pinch pennies or think twice about which airline you'd use, at which hotel you'd stay, or where to find the most satisfying meals for your bucks. Unfortunately, you–like most other small business owners–must discover ways to travel farther for fewer dollars, because it's you who are picking up the tab. Fortunately, however, there are a number of corners you can cut without feeling like you're going steerage.

One of the largest expenses you'll encounter is transportation to the market site, New York, perhaps, or Los Angeles, Dallas, Atlanta, or wherever. Unless you live within a couple of hundred miles of the market city, you'll no doubt want to fly there, since your time is very precious. Traveling by train or bus is obviously a false economy because it takes so much longer. So that leaves you trying to find the lowest airfare available.

Several companies market travel savings through the "club" concept. That is, you pay an annual fee–usually from $25 to $75–and thereby become eligible for discounted travel services. American Leisure Industries operates several such clubs, including Encore, a travel service that charges $36 a year and has more than a million members. Call (800) 638-0930 for details about Encore's "second night free" lodging plan and other travel bargains, including airfare and rental cars. You can save the cost of membership in just one or two trips by asking for the absolutely cheapest airfare available at the time you need to travel.

Other discount travel groups include the American Travel Association in Westerville, Ohio (800-553-8500); Vacations To Go in Houston (800-624-7338); Impulse in Englewood, Colorado (800-251-8853); McTravel Travel Services in Northbrook, Illinois (800-331-2941); and Discount Travel International in Naberth, Pennsylvania (215-668-2182).

American Leisure also offers the Ultimate Travel Network, a program for both business and leisure travelers. Membership in the Network costs between about $85 and $115 and is distributed by Amway. Their officials are reluctant to reveal details of the program, but suggest if you'd like to compare their benefits against those of, say, Encore, just call an Amway distributor listed in your white pages.

You may also want to investigate the National Travel Club. Membership in that group costs about $15 a year and entitles you to a subscription to *Travel Holiday* magazine, travel accident insurance, trip routing service, and discounts on car rentals and books. Each of these groups claims to offer some feature that the others don't, so you'll want to explore several of them before deciding which one will save you the most money.

If you're older than 55, you'll find you can save--sometimes a great deal--on hotel expenses. Omni Hotels, for example, offer a 50 percent discount to members of the American Association of Retired Persons (AARP). Ramada Inns and Sheraton Hotels give a 25 percent discount to AARP members and other senior groups. Many, many chains extend smaller--10 to 15 percent--discounts to the same groups of travelers. It will pay you to inquire about discounts when you book reservations at any hotel or motel chain in the country, if you are older or a member of some special group.

Still another way to save on lodging expense is to read ads in the newspapers of the cities you'll be visiting. For example, the Milford Plaza (a Best Western Hotel), Hotel Esplanade, and the Marriott Marquis--all in New York City--have special rates for apparel trade travelers. Check your yellow pages for toll-free phone numbers. As might be expected, *Women's Wear Daily* is a good source of information about hotel bargains in New York.

However, discounted airfares and hotel rooms aren't the only savings you can effect if you really have to travel on a shoestring. (And going to market is so important for your business that if traveling cheaply is the only way you can manage, it's worth the scrimping.) Take along an immersion heater or small electric pot for boiling water in your room, and a small jar of instant coffee. Then you can manage a respectable breakfast for peanuts. Orange juice will stay nicely chilled if you buy a small container before you tuck in for the night and stow it in a bucket of ice until morning. If you've carried a small pack of cold cereal from home, you can enjoy it with a carton of milk kept overnight in the bathroom sink filled with ice. A breakfast roll or doughnut from a nearby bakery or deli will also help keep hunger pangs at bay until lunch time and help you save as much as $10 a day on breakfasts.

If you yearn to sample the famous restaurants in the city you're visiting, do it for lunch. Without exception, the cost of lunches is far smaller than that of dinners-- often for the same food. If your budget rules out even lunch at an elegant eatery, find a deli or bakery that will make sandwiches for you. Then walk to the nearest park or other place where you can sit down to enjoy both your meal and the passing scene. Often this trick serves as a tension-reliever as well as a budget aid.

Many times when you're away from home you like to unwind with a drink or glass of wine before dinner. Or perhaps you'd like to ask a couple of new friends to join you for a drink. If you go into the hotel bar, you can expect to pay *at the very least* four or five dollars per drink. On the other hand, a whole bottle of nice wine will set you back less than ten. Or you might want to consider toting a bottle of vodka or gin from home and mixing it with soda you pick up at a nearby liquor store, deli, or hotel soft-drink machine.

If you like to nibble when you drink, include in your suitcase a can of salted nuts and a box of cheese crackers or some such. With the addition of Perrier or other nonalcoholic beverage, you can manage a very respectable cocktail gathering for people you've met during the day. If you picked up the tab for three or four at a bar, you'd spend $50 at least.

Another way your travel dollars dribble away without your even noticing is in tips. You can't get out of tipping the cabbie or restaurant server, but you can avoid paying the skycap and bellman. Be sure your luggage is on wheels--either the built-in kind or the little frames that flight attendants tug so jauntily as they stride through airports. And if your carry-on bag is light enough to be slung over your shoulder, you'll never need to pay someone else to carry your bags. When you need a cab, walk some distance from the hotel entrance to hail your own. You'll escape having to give the doorman 50 cents or a dollar just for blowing his whistle. You can probably save as much as $20 each trip by not handing out tips quite so freely.

Make use of a shuttle service or airport bus when getting to and from the airport. You'll save at least five dollars a day in parking fees. In New York City, if several of you share a cab from Kennedy or La Guardia, it will cost you about what you'd spend on their less-than-ideal shuttle services. On the other hand, in Los Angeles and many other cities, the SUPER SHUTTLE will whisk you efficiently, economically, and in comfort to and from the airport.

Plan your market trips carefully to uncover other ways to save that add up to big bucks. You may be pleasantly surprised to find that you can manage to go to market more often.

SECTION X: COMPUTERS

Chapter Forty-six:
EVERYONE NEEDS
A COMPUTER?

Does your family *need* a car? The answer has to be no, since families survived for thousands of years before the invention of the automobile. Will a car make your family's life more comfortable and satisifying? Of course. If you were to ask, "Does my business *need* a computer?" the answer would again be no. Until just the last 30 years or so businesses prospered without help from computers. Will a computer make your business more profitable? Possibly. But don't expect a computer to revive a business that's in financial trouble. Installing a computer could make the trouble worse by adding a host of new problems. However, a computer can help a healthy, thriving business grow to even greater prosperity.

Before you shout, "That's for me," take a good look at where your business is and what you hope to accomplish through computerization. First, consider these questions: Are your gross yearly sales at least $500,000? Do you have a large file of customers and accounts receivable? Does it take several days to get your statements out each month? Do you have problems controlling your inventory? Does routine paperwork take up a large portion of your time? If you answer "yes" to all or most of these questions, your business would probably benefit from the addition of a computer system.

Because computers seem to do everything, we sometimes forget that there are many areas in which they are of no help at all. A computer won't get new customers; it won't supply creative solutions to your business problems; it probably won't solve a problem you couldn't solve without it; it can't systematize your operation if you don't already have a good system. And if you aren't detail-oriented, don't expect a computer installation to work. You'll have to pay more attention to the way you do your record keeping than you did with a manual system. Computers are unforgiving of sloppy record entry and mistakes.

Remember, too, that the computer is the least expensive element of a business system; the people who operate it are the most expensive. Even the most carefully designed computer system will demand a lot of somebody's time. You'll encounter a host of hidden expenses, also, when you computerize. You and your employees will have to spend a fair amount of time learning how to use the new system. The computer will have to go down for maintenance from time to time and it will occasionally go down out of sheer contrariness. In most parts of the country you'll have to pay property tax on the computer equipment, and, of course, you'll want special insurance on all that fancy machinery.

If, after considering all these caveats, you still believe a computer will help your business meet today's challenges, how will you go about setting it up? Your first task will be to locate the software–instructions to the computer-that will perform the jobs you want done. Don't let some slick computer salesman tell you to select your machine first; the first order of business in designing a computer system is choosing programs that will produce the forms and reports you need. Talk to other retailers; ask them what software they use. Read trade publications for possible help. Try to talk to at least three retailers with successful computer installations, ones that are performing the tasks expected, with the least amount of human intervention and the fewest problems.

Consult the experts who really know how information is processed in your own business. Who are they? The people who do the work now. No one knows better than your own employees how various jobs are done and what problems accompany each task. Getting your employees involved in early decisions will help them overcome their natural aversion to change, too, and make them more cooperative.

Never forget that information is the life blood of your business. Each day you have to deal with bills to be paid, letters to suppliers, invoices, inventory tags, letters urging new customers to visit your store, and a host of other bits of paper that define your store's activities. A computer can help you with those chores, but don't expect overnight change. You and your employees will feel awkward with it at first; sometimes you and they will make mistakes that are difficult to correct. With patient persistence, however, all of you will soon accept the computer for what it is: a very handy tool to help you keep up with the storm of paper necessary to keep your business growing.

Chapter Forty-seven:
SOFTWARE

A thoroughly unscientific and random study has revealed that owners of apparel stores in Los Angeles, at least, aren't taking advantage of the electronic assistance available to them. Of about 15 stores polled, only one reported using software specially designed to help apparel store managers keep their businesses on the right track. Several said they are equipped with point-of-sale cash registers that do some of the myriad chores necessary for inventory keeping and printing customers' receipts, but little else. It would appear that smaller stores, the very ones who could make the best use of programs designed for sellers of women's fashions, are resisting investing in computerware.

Let's take a look at the feast of electronic helpers that is available to you. Even if you believe the cost is beyond your resources, you won't have to lay out a cent to see a demonstration of some of the latest goodies.

"You're the Boss" is retail management software created by Coleman & Wright Software, a division of East End Computers, Inc. "If you're a retailer and want to computerize," says the firm's brochure, "but don't want a computer taking over your business, you're going to like our program." The flyer says "You're the Boss" was designed to be flexible. It can serve as a point-of-sale program with a cash drawer, or as a back-office system, or everything can be tied together so that the bills can go out as inventory is being received and as sales are being made. You can print receipts or not; you can track commissions or not. You can discount any item by a percentage and/or by a dollar amount. You can get sales reports at the end of each day, or any time you feel like it. It will keep track of inventory for you, producing MTD and YTD sales figures on any item or group of items. And the number of items you can deal with is limited only by disk space. The system will flag reorder points, but doesn't print purchase orders.

"Boss" does print envelopes, labels, and post cards, as well as letters, and lists. It sorts lists of customers by zip code or any other criteria you choose. Phyllis Wright, spokeswoman for Coleman & Wright, says the software is available all over the country. Just call (800) 453-6767 to find out where you can see it in action.

Mike Paradiso, spokesman for Egghead Stores--the K Mart of software distributors--says his company has received a point-of-sale program that sells for $250. He says it was formerly known as "Cash Register," but now is called P.O.S. It will print receipts, keep track of inventory, flag reorder points. You can even buy for $350 an optional cash drawer to attach to your IBM compatible personal computer, thereby turning your PC into a P.O.S. cash register.

Paradiso says Egghead stores also carry wands for reading bar codes. He recommends that you read a book titled *I.B.M. PC Expansion and Software Guide*, published by Que Corp.; 7999 Knue Road; Indianapolis, IN 46250, to learn more about what's on the shelves at stores like his.

Mitchell Jamel, president of Mr. Software, Apparel Software in Los Angeles says his firm custom designs systems for small stores. "We are the small store's solution," Jamel says, "to getting exactly what they need and can afford." Their application packages start at about $1,000 and run as high as $7,000. "But it's like having another very smart, very dedicated employee," says Jamel. One of Mr. Software's outstanding packages is "Elite," a system that "does everything," including purchase orders, and open to buy. The firm is at 112 Ninth Street, Suite 309, Los Angeles 90015.

If you're looking for an electronic way to maintain your mailing list, you may want to look into "WHO," distributed by Robotronics; 7800 MacArthur Blvd.; Oakland, CA 94605. WHO can address reports, maintain address and phone lists, print 3 x 5 file cards, 2 x 4 cards for your rotary file, labels, letters. With a hard disk computer it will hold 32,000 names, or 1,000 on a double-sided, double density floppy disk. WHO comes in MS-DOS and CP/M versions and sells for $99.

Perhaps you need taskware that is even less expensive. Look into "Checks & Balances," a single-entry accounting system that allows you to balance your checkbook, print checks, produce profit and loss statements, produce a net worth statement, and flag tax-related items. The program can also track income and expenses for tax purposes with 128 user-defined categories. Available for CP/M, MS-DOS. Contact CDE Software; 948 Tularosa Drive; Los Angeles, CA 90026.

It's obvious that the times they are a-changing, and you don't want to be left behind. Small computers that will do much--if not all--of your bookkeeping drudgery for just a pittance more than a song are available everywhere. Software to run them is equally ubiquitous. Enlist the aid of a friend who is well-versed in computer lore and go in search of the software that can make your life so much easier.

Chapter Forty-eight:
QR--BOON
OR BUZZWORD?

Is *Quick Response* just another of those buzzwords that show up from time to time in all industries? You hear it being tossed around at shows and seminars or any other place where members of the textile, apparel, and retail industries get together. But does QR really hold promise for small store owners who can't afford to invest millions in new equipment?

Originally planned as a strategy to help American manufacturers beat back the recent invasion of imported textile products, QR has proved to be a boon to retailers, too. According to Peter W. Harding of Kurt Salmon Associates, "Quick Response (QR) has already made history in the apparel business, but the best is yet to come." And Al Zindel, president of Jantzen's women's division says, "Before [QR], by the time you found out an item was hot, it was too late to make any more." Of course, he speaks from a supplier's point of view, but the same thing can be said by retailers: Before Quick Response technology the hottest-selling fashion items couldn't be reordered because of long lead and delivery times. Another expert in the industry says EDI (electronic data interchange, the operations that make QR work) might have saved the apparel industry from shooting itself in the foot over short skirts.

Exactly what is this QR that is supposed to be the salvation of all segments of the apparel industry? Quick Response and its partner EDI are nothing more--nor less--than new technologies that shorten reorder times, thereby reducing inventories, stockouts, and markdowns. EDI is simply a method of letting computers do the talking. On one end computers transmit purchase orders, as well as other critical data, generated electronically at a retail outlet to a supplier, where they are received by a computer and placed in the manufacturing or shipping stream by computers.

Making both technologies feasible are bar codes, those black-and-white blocks of lines both thick and thin, you've been seeing for years on cans of tomatoes, books, bags of salad greens, almost anything you've bought in a supermarket. An article in *Women's Wear Daily* reported that as long ago as 1987 apparel retailers were pressing for bar codes to be applied to garments by manufacturers.

In that article William Sumner, vice president of information systems at

Bullock's, Los Angeles, was quoted as saying, "What we're talking about is a campaign for interindustry self-improvement. It's not one but a group of standards and technologies." He added, "The bottom line is making it work for both vendors and retailers." At that time only about five to ten percent of merchandise arriving at Bullock's stores was bar coded at the source. That figure grows each day, according to other retailers. K Mart, for example, expects to have all its vendors putting bar codes on their products by 1990.

Quick Response begins with tracking goods--everything from shirts to dresses--by means of bar codes printed on hang tags. Scanning those codes (which usually identify items by color, size, maker, and so on) lets stores keep a close eye on what's moving and what's not. This information is relayed back to the supplier or manufacturer by EDI. As merchandise sells, reorder messages are sent by computer to the supplier who, in turn, relays the information to the manufacturer. Thus, new supplies can be received in a matter of days, instead of weeks.

Some of the retailers who sell garments made by Haggar Apparel Company, for example, count on computers, not human employees, to regulate shipments they receive from the Dallas-based firm. Bar code scanners at retail outlets let the company's distributors know exactly what each retailer sells. The distributor sends regular shipments to each retailer, keeping in-store inventory at predetermined levels.

On the other side of the cycle, Haggar is linked to its own fabric suppliers, using a similar bar-coding scheme, so raw materials are used in Haggar factories as quickly as finished clothing moves to retailers. Inventory in Haggar warehouses is thus kept to a minimum, according to Gary Swank, vice president of operations.

Retailers benefit from such QR activities because their inventories are kept to a profitable minimum without risking stockouts and still reducing markdowns. In theory, the new technology will also do away with the need to take physical inventory counts, make writing reorders a thing of the past, and reduce the risk of cash flow problems caused by slow-moving inventory.

Some retailing experts insist that quick response will work for basic goods stocked all year round, but never for trendy fashion goods since there isn't time to reorder such items. Detractors of QR also accurately point out that frequent ordering can lead to higher freight costs. But QR supporters insist that slightly elevated shipping expenses will be soon recaptured by increased turnover.

At Personal, a division of Leslie Fay, a three-month trial of QR involving a basic line of pants, skirts, and jackets yielded an extra $250,000 in reorders. Alan Golub, president of Leslie Fay, says he was skeptical when news of QR first started spreading about three years ago. Saying he was sure it would never work in the fashion industry, he admits a trial in his company's Haberdashery line made a believer out of him. "My feeling," Golub says, "is in five years you're going to have bar coding on everything."

Bob Salem, president of Counterparts, New York, agrees. He says he thinks bar codes will benefit fashion lines because of the precise information they yield. "There is too much margin for error," he notes, "by doing it manually." He points out that bar coding will let retailers capture every bit of information about every single sale and make it possible for them to use that knowledge when planning for the future.

How will small stores take advantage of this exciting new technology? Richard Widney, vice president of marketing for Retail Merchandising Service Automation, Inc., says, "For a couple of thousand dollars a small retailer can get a small personal computer and a modem (the little gadget you hook up to your phone to let your computer talk to another one at a distant location) to gather your sales information and send it off to be processed."

An outside data processing service (sometimes called a service bureau) is the answer for store owners who don't want (and cannot afford) to get involved with computer-savvy employees, hardware, software, and all the rest. Most cities have at least one such service that in just a few hours, or overnight, crunches the numbers you send via a phone line and returns resulting information the same way. One processor that caters exclusively to the apparel industry is Commercial On-Line Systems of New York. Maxway Data Corporation is a New York firm that is seeking clients in the fashion industry. "It's one way to start without having to employ people who are experienced in [computers]," says Arthur Valentine, vice president at Wendy Gell.

Retailers who work with Maxway don't even have to worry about having a terminal and modem in their stores. For Maxway does "batch processing," which deals with paper records collected at the store and sent to the data center. This process is somewhat slower than the COLS on-line system, but eliminates the need for extensive training for data entry personnel. According to some users, on-line processing can be expensive because of the need for long--if not continuous--phone connections. RMSA's Richard Widney suggests that on-line data transmission probably isn't for you if your annual gross sales aren't at least half a million dollars.

But that's not to say you cannot take advantage of QR technologies. Look in your yellow pages for data processing services that may make it all work for you. Contact several. The biggest are IBM's Information Network and GE Information Services, but don't discount smaller companies that might be eager to work with small retailers. Ask for price quotes, demonstrations, plain language explanations of what each service can do for you. If a large part of your merchandise arrives at your store with bar-coded hang tags, you're ready to enter the electronic age, even if your budget won't permit a big up-front investment.

Chapter Forty-nine:
AI--FACT OR FANTASY?

According to some "whiz-kid" types, artificial intelligence (AI) is on the verge of transforming the way we do business. "Smart" computers, we're told, will soon replace factory workers, managers, even doctors. According to Beau Sheil, director of artificial intelligence at the Price Waterhouse Technology Centre in Menlo Park, California, AI is still a long way from delivering on the more extravagant claims that have been made for it.

We've all heard of computers that are unbeatable at checkers, says Sheil. All it takes is a computer program that contains all the move choices a player has at any point in the game. It's a huge task, getting all that knowledge into a computer, but the number of options is finite. Consider, on the other hand, trying to program a computer to answer the telephone, regarded as a simple task. It takes only a few sentences to tell another person how to do it. But, clearly, answering the phone is more complicated than playing checkers, because an almost unbounded number of topics and activities can be introduced in the course of a phone conversation. Dealing with them all requires an enormous breadth of knowledge.

Actually, it's an "expert system" that tells the machine how to play checkers or diagnose illness or make routine retailing decisions. "We feel expert systems are an exciting concept and there are a lot of applications for them," says Kathy Spangenberg, director of systems and programming for Mervyn's, a department store chain headquartered in Hayward, California.

According to Clark Holloway and Herbert Hand, professors at the College of Business Administration of the University of South Carolina, an expert system is a sophisticated computer program that can analyze a situation in a particular field (such as medicine, oil exploration, or business). The expert system can produce sophisticated results faster, and often better, than its human counterpart.

Steve Chenoweth, a consulting systems analyst, says expert systems could be used for merchandise planning, training, even product selection and promotion. However, he cautioned, "fashion merchandising may be too fuzzy in some cases even for AI."

Retailing experts of RMSA (Retail Merchandising Service Automation, Inc.), a California firm that specializes in finding solutions to retailers' problems, caution that computers are mere tools that cannot replace the human ability to make complex decisions. A computer is not swayed by personal likes, RMSA points out.

If you were to allow a computer program to select your merchandise, for example, it would search your history files and select garments from lines that sold well in the past. What the computer is lacking, however, is a fashion sense--or intuition--that recognizes that styles and fabrics that were hot last year may be losers this year. Computers possessing the ability to make that kind of decision are still many years in the future. Computer capability available to retail operations today is extremely logical and pragmatic.

According to the experts at RMSA, if you are considering letting automation do your thinking, or expect it to perform magic, you're going to end up with tainted decisions. People cannot yet be fully replaced by machines, but computers can accrue, accumulate, and store vast amounts of history and make this information available in usable formats with uncanny speed.

Other industry consultants insist expert systems should not be ignored by retailers. They say the tight labor market and intense competition make retailing an ideal arena for exploiting a computer's ability to help people make astute decisions.

At a recent convention sponsored by the National Retail Merchants Association, several software developers reported that they were building expert systems for store management. Coopers & Lybrand has developed for one client a markdown system designed to cut the time it takes to figure what prices to lower. "It lets buyers engage in a more strategic approach," says Helen Oijha, director of the group that developed the expert system.

Creative Data Systems of Cleveland is presently devising a commercial version of the markdown system for basic, seasonal and high-fashion merchandise. That system, however, will be intended for retailers whose annual sales range from $25 million to $400 million. An expert system designed to run on personal computers is in the works at Retail Mate Corporation of Wilmington, Delaware. This system will handle planning, distribution, monitoring sales, and replenishment. Since shoppers' top priority is finding quality goods fast, Joseph Coates--who runs a Washington policy research group--advises retailers to maintain profiles of their customers and purchases in order to recommend merchandise.

A Canadian company, Retail Solutions, Inc., sells a computer program called "The Retailer" that works with POS (point-of-sale) terminals and computers. It takes merchants into a world of instantaneous inventory control, automatic ordering, and easy bookkeeping. This expert system, which has been installed in more than 4,000 retail outlets in Canada and the U.S., costs about $3,000. It will run on almost any IBM compatible with a hard disk memory and will handle input from terminals, cash registers, or even remote stores via a modem. According to a recent article in *Canadian Business*, while sales are going on out front, the accountant can be reading an up-to-the-minute general ledger, the owner can compare purchase orders, gross margins and receivables, and a clerk can be printing out bar-code price tags to be read by an optical scanner at the checkout. The system keeps track of credit card authorizations, serial numbers, and customer accounts, too.

One retailer relying extensively on expert systems is Mrs. Fields, Inc., the Utah-based cookie maker. Personal computers in each outlet of the chain continually monitor sales, identify trends and direct operations every hour, instructing managers how much dough to mix and how many cookies to bake. Another program even reviews employment applications. "I don't know how we could operate without it," says Paul Quinn, vice president for management information systems.

Carter Hawley Hale, operator of nearly 300 retail stores, has been implementing a computer system for more than four years. The corporation uses about 560 IBM PCs, in addition to thousands of IBM terminals and POS terminals, to centralize the large chain's activities. Besides serving as internal communicators, the PCs are being linked up with manufacturers and distributors of CHH merchandise. The system enables the company to place its orders instantly and electronically, instead of having to depend on the much slower mail.

Peter R. Johnson & Associates, Inc., of Greenbrae, California, is creating a "buyer workstation" that recommends how to buy and distribute basic and seasonal merchandise.

Many of these expert systems are now affordable for small businesses and they are rapidly becoming essential if small stores are to compete with the large operators. Specialty stores have always had the advantage of being able to respond to customers' needs and changing tastes more quickly than cumbersome chains with their layers of bureaucracy. But that edge is being eroded by expert systems that make even the largest retailers as flexible as a single store. Thus, to remain ahead in the race for customer favor, independents will have to learn to make use of the benefits of the age of artificial intelligence.

SECTION XI:
ODDS AND ENDS

Chapter Fifty:
HOW TO BEAT THE CLOCK

If you run short of money, you can call on a bank to lend you more. If your merchandise gets low, vendors will replace it in a hurry. If you run out of room in your store, you can move or enlarge. But what can you do when you run out of time? You can't borrow more or draw on hours saved in the past. You must make the most of the 1,440 minutes you are allotted each day. How you fill those minutes will be a big factor in determining whether your store is a success or failure.

Time-management experts say some of the most often cited time wasters are telephone calls; meetings; visitors; emergencies; dealing with personal problems of employees; trying to do too much at once; failure to say no; not delegating responsibility. The most efficient managers are those who have found ways to control these and other time wasters.

To discover how to manage your time better you'll need to gain an accurate picture of how you are currently spending it. Block out a grid with either 15- or 30-minute intervals and write down what you have accomplished within each time frame. Chart your activities for a week, rating each one as 1, 2, or 3 in terms of importance. If your work varies widely, you may want to chart two or three very different weeks. Once you have an accurate record of where your time goes, you can identify your own time wasters and delete unnecessary tasks while revealing all that can be delegated.

Next, make a "to-do" list each day, listing tasks in order of descending importance. As you accomplish each chore, cross it off. Don't work on anything else until the topmost item remaining on the list is finished. Don't add a new task to today's list, but start one for tomorrow. Any task that is left over at day's end also goes on tomorrow's list.

If possible, let someone else answer the phone, screening callers for you. Post a list of people for whom you will interrupt your work a) at any time (the mayor, for example) or b) in an emergency (your children or spouse probably show up on this list). If you are expecting a call, remember to temporarily add that person's name to your list.

Outgoing calls can be time-wasters, too, unless you plan them carefully. Before you place a call, note on a card the facts you want to cover and questions you need to ask. Jot the answers on the same card and you have a written record of the call. End the call when your list is exhausted.

When you have to receive a call, try to keep it brief. If the caller is seeking information, make notes on a card and promise to call back when you have the necessary facts; don't try to look things up while the caller waits. Jot the requested data on the card and use it to control the length of time it takes to return the call. If a personal call slips through the screening process, firmly tell the caller what your working hours are and invite him or her to call you at home.

Meetings can be time thieves, too. You do have to meet with your salespeople often, but have in hand a list of the topics you want to cover and don't let the meeting become a coffee klatch. If personnel problems come up, arrange to meet later with the people involved, but don't let these problems take over the meeting.

Don't become a parental figure or a shoulder for your employees to cry on. Be sympathetic, of course, in the face of a death in the family or serious illness, but don't get entangled in lovers' spats, family quarrels, and so on.

Recognize that you don't have to finish in one fell swoop every task you start. Break chores down into little pieces, where possible. You may be able to accomplish some of the pieces while you wait in the dentist's office or when riding the bus to work. If, on the other hand, a chore must be completed at once--a tax report, say, or an order for merchandise--insist that you be allowed to do it. Accept no calls or visitors; brook no interruptions short of a fire in the building. You might want to consider setting aside one block of such time each week.

Get to your desk an hour or two early on days when your to-do list is unusually long. If you find yourself saying, "I don't have time" too often, you may want to make it a practice to get to work ahead of everyone else one day each week. You'll find you can accomplish a great deal when no employees or customers are in the store.

These early hours might be the ideal time to tackle chores you don't particularly like. Do you hate doing bookkeeping, for example? If so, be sure to schedule that task early in the day when your energy is high. Also, left until the end of the day, disliked bits of work are more easily postponed and can seem to hang over you like a threat, sapping your enthusiasm for other tasks.

Try to vary each day's work--and each week's. Nothing grows boring so quickly as doing the same things at the same time, day after day. Build flexibility into your schedule: leave blocks of time open for coping with crises or going for a walk in the mall to check the competition.

Postpone taking your lunch hour until 1 p.m. or so, when restaurants won't be so crowded. Avoid, if possible, "working lunches." They can be stressful and you need to relax during the time you're away from the store.

And remember that even the best time-savers won't work all the time. You will find yourself running out of time during big promotions. Sometimes you will want to let a meeting run on while you listen to your employees exchange ideas. And once in a while you'll want to chat on the phone during business hours. If you recognize that these are time-wasting events, you won't let them become habits again and you'll be making the most of your time.

Chapter Fifty-one:
MEET THE HMO
FOR SMALL BUSINESS

Most business people regard the Small Business Administration (SBA) as a trauma center, a place to turn for help when their businesses are at death's door or when they are about to give birth to new endeavors. But the SBA was really designed to be an HMO, health maintenance organization, for small businesses. The SBA stands ready to lend a hand in getting new businesses off the ground, to show their owners how to keep successful businesses flourishing, and to offer options to shutting down when a business gets into trouble.

Created in 1953, the SBA is the only federal agency whose sole charge is to provide service to owners of small businesses. SBA's mission is counsel, assist, and protect the interests of small business; to ensure that small business concerns receive a fair portion of government purchases and contracts. Further, SBA must make sure that when government property is sold, small business owners have a chance to buy a fair share of it. It's widely known that the SBA also makes loans to small business owners, but the limitations and circumstances of those loans are often not understood.

Here, then, is a listing and brief explanation of help you can receive from your government, through the Small Business Administration.

Business loans. SBA has helped thousands of small companies get started, expand, and prosper through two basic types of business loans: 1) guaranty loans made by private lenders, usually banks, and guaranteed up to 90 percent by SBA; and 2) direct loans. Most SBA loans are of the guaranty type. Direct loans are available only to applicants unable to secure SBA-guaranteed loans. Before applying for a direct loan, an applicant must seek financing from her own bank and, in large cities, from at least one other lender. Direct loan funds are very limited.

Applicants for either type of loan must be of good character, demonstrate sufficient management expertise and commitment to run a successful operation, and have enough capital to operate on a sound financial basis. For new businesses, this includes sufficient resources, when loan proceeds are combined with personal capital, to withstand start-up expenses and the initial operating phase during which losses are likely to occur. To qualify as a small business, a retail operation must have receipts that do not exceed $3.5 to $13.5 million, depending on the industry. To learn more about the SBA loan program, call your nearest local Small Business Administration office (there are more than a hundred such branches in cities large and small throughout the country) and ask for the free brochure *Business Loans from the SBA.*

Prebusiness Workshops. These are the SBA's main educational programs for aspiring entrepreneurs and usually last one day or several evenings. The workshops target those seeking to start quite small retail and service businesses. Participants with even a modicum of business sophistication complain that these workshops are too basic. They are offered on a continuing basis and are free.

Management counseling. Small business owners are in constant need of new information, feedback on the condition of their operations, and counseling to help them improve their management skills. To accomplish these ends, the SBA maintains a number of resource programs to counsel small business people in the areas of marketing, buying, producing, selling, recordkeeping, financial management, financing, and administration.

One of these programs is SCORE (Service Corps of Retired Executives), composed of thousands of retired business executives who volunteer to help small business owners solve their problems. SBA tries to match the needs of a particular business with the expertise of a SCORE volunteer who will make a detailed analysis of the business and devise a plan to help.

The collective experience of SCORE volunteers spans the full range of American management, including office managers, accountants, advertising and public relations experts, and sales managers. SCORE's free service is specifically designed to help the small entrepreneur who cannot afford to pay for professional assistance. Some critics say that, since most SCORE volunteers come from large-company backgrounds, they may not fully understand the different needs and problems of small business. Also, these critics claim, because they are retired, SCORE members may use business methods that are outdated. However, since the advice is free, you won't go too far astray by seeking counseling from SCORE.

Another counseling program deemed by many to be more up-to-date is ACE, Active Corps of Executives, a cadre of more than 2,500 practicing business managers. Organized in 1969 to supplement the SCORE program, ACE volunteers are recruited from major industry, trade associations, educational institutions, and professions. Mid-career executives form the ranks of the group and are used on an as-needed basis. These volunteers share current business understanding with the community and increase their own executive-level experience by working in the ACE program. Their service is free.

The third facet in SBA's management counseling system is SBI, the Small Business Institute, begun in 1972. This program is a three-way cooperative among more than 500 collegiate schools of business administration, members of the country's small business community, and the SBA. Under the supervision of university faculty and SBA staff, MBA candidates work directly with the owners of small firms to give them on-site counseling at no charge. SBI serves both as an educational tool for business students and a consulting service for small business owners. However, businesses are not automatically accepted for SBI help. They are screened by professors with an eye to ensuring that both students and business owners will benefit.

Quick help is not a product of the SBI program. The consulting is performed over one semester, which usually lasts ten to thirteen weeks. Still, small business operators seem to be pleased with the SBI program.

To obtain counseling service for your business, call the SBA office listed in your telephone directory. In some large cities, SCORE has its own listing in the U.S. Government section.

Practical, hands-on training. A 1982 survey of small business owners revealed that one of the greatest needs of the small business community is management training adapted to the small business environment and available locally. SBA has developed a network of institutions and trainers to deliver this type of training. Among the offerings are introductory training for prospective business owners and uninformed new owners. Topics covered usually include Personality Traits Needed, Management Skills, Success and Failure Factors, Market Analysis, Legal Aspects, Recordkeeping, Financial Factors, Sources of Capital, Regulations, Taxes, and Insurance. This training is usually presented in a single-day workshop format. SBA also presents a follow-up program for prebusiness participants who want further instruction. For details contact the Office of Management Information and Training, Management Assistance; Small Business Administration; 1522 K Street N.W.; Room 626; Washington, DC 20416, or call your local SBA office.

Still another aspect of SBA's management training program is "Back to Basics" skill training. This program is targeted to both new and established owners who need training. It provides participants with practical skills to use in identifying and solving problems in their own businesses. Standard units usually include: 1) small business management; 2) business planning for the small firm; 3) marketing and sales in small business (half of what business is all about: selling); 4) purchasing and cost control for small business (buying: the other half of what business is all about); 5) small business recordkeeping and its use; 6) financial management for small business; 7) legal and risk management: how to protect what you've built. These topics are normally presented as a group of short, noncredit courses or as multiday conferences.

Other, specialized training is offered by SBA in more advanced aspects of managing small business. Topics offered in this program can be grouped in four categories. They are: 1) function-related (such as inventory control, pricing, or micro-computers); 2) industry-related, applying to certain types of business (such as retail, service, artists); 3) time-related, referring to new tax laws (for example, survival during an economic downswing); and 4) special emphasis training for designated groups (such as minorities, women, veterans, handicapped persons).

SBA sponsors these workshops with community colleges, universities, vocational schools, chambers of commerce, trade associations, and a host of other entities.

Management publications. Dozens of management assistance pamphlets are available for a very small price from the SBA. They deal with functional problems in the areas of financial management and analysis, planning, marketing, administration, personnel, government affairs. For a complete listing write to U.S. Small Business Administration; P.O. Box 30; Denver, CO 80201-0300. Ask for pamphlet 115. It's free. Or call your local SBA office and ask them to send it to you.

For somewhat larger prices, but still good values, you can buy booklets in the "Small Business Management Series." They include such titles as *Management Audit for Small Retailers, Small Store Planning for Growth* and *Retail Merchandise Management.* Prices range from about $3.50 to $6.50.

Small Business Answer Desk. By far the most versatile source of help offered by the SBA is its 800-number referral service. This "hot line" taps the expertise of SBA professionals and directs callers to government agencies, trade associations, or other appropriate resources. The toll-free number for the answer desk is (800) 368-5855. It is staffed Monday through Friday from 9 am to 5 pm.

If your business isn't as robust as you'd like, get in touch with the Small Business Administration. It's a good bet one of the agency's programs will enable you to administer the remedies your business needs to prosper.

Chapter Fifty-two:
MISTAKES YOU'LL
WANT TO AVOID

Do you ever take note of obvious mistakes made by owners of other retail stores in your mall or area? Do you ever wonder what errors--if any--you and your employees commit each day? If you don't examine your business--both its physical aspects and the way it serves customers--with a critical eye from time to time, you're in danger of growing complacent. No business operator does everything right, every day. And the best way for you to discover what it is you're doing that might offend customers and subtract from your profits is to ask. Ask your customers, in an informal survey or by means of a suggestion box. Ask your friends if you've grown careless in the conduct of your business; urge them to be honest. Especially, ask your competition. Of course, the owner of the specialty store down the block isn't going to say to you, "As a matter of fact, I did notice. . . ."

Getting help from competitors isn't quite that simple, but it's not really hard. Let someone else take over your store for a few hours each day for a week or two. Then spend the time you've freed up visiting other stores, shopping like an ordinary consumer. Make notes of the things that cause you discomfort or discourage you from buying. When you get back to your store, analyze your findings to see how many of those competitors' mistakes have crept into your own way of doing business. It will be a revelation.

Here are some of the problems you're likely to uncover. First, is your store arrangement off-putting? Have you squeezed in one more rounder, added another special rack until shoppers can't get into the store? If you cater to young women who are likely to be shopping with children in strollers, can they push through easily? Don't make it easier for potential customers to pass you by than to look at the merchandise you have on display.

Have you allowed your employees to decide what background music will be played on the radio, instead of insisting on a station appropriate for your clientele? Is the music so loud that customers must shout to make their needs known?

Has your store grown dingy without your noticing? Do your mannequins have dirty--or cracked or chipped--faces? If they have any broken parts, have them repaired if you can afford the cost or retire them. Substitute newer, more modern-looking wall fixtures and slat-work. Be sure dust hasn't collected on any of your fixtures or furnishings. If you have dusty artificial flower arrangements on counters or tables, trash them. They're not worth saving.

Have you grown slack about washing your store windows (or having it done) every other day or so? Nothing turns shoppers off more quickly than sticky handprints coming between them and your window displays.

Does a clutter of signs fill much of your window space? Sure, it's good business to give community groups a boost by putting news of their activities in the window, but don't forget to remove the signs as soon as the date is past. It might be prudent, also, to develop a policy of limiting such announcements to one or two at a time and none when you have your own announcements or SALE banners in the window.

If you and the only salesperson on the floor are busy with customers when the phone rings, does one of you excuse herself to answer it? If so, you're making one of the mistakes shoppers dislike most. Why should the bird in the hand (as it were) be less important than the one in the bush (or on the phone)? When you dash away to answer the phone you give your customer two things: 1) the feeling that any caller is more important to you than she is, and 2) the time to decide she'd rather shop elsewhere. If you can't bear to let the phone ring, you might want to have an answering machine that's programed to answer after the fourth or fifth ring with something like, "Sorry, we're all busy helping customers right now. Please call again in a few minutes or leave your number and we'll call you as soon as possible."

When you and your staff are counting or rearranging stock, do you expect customers to wait for help until one of you finishes a certain item or counter? Or do you simply point to the area where the requested garment is to be found? Before you start on a housekeeping chore, be sure at least one salesperson has been assigned to drop everything to greet shoppers. Nothing is more important than attending to the needs of customers.

Have you allowed your staff to fall into the bad habit of finishing personal conversations before they go to the assistance of a shopper? Whether the conversation is being conducted personally or on the phone, it should cease mid-word when a customer appears. In fact, it might be good policy to forbid personal calls and conversations at all times. In these days of expensive help, why should you pay people to chat?

It's a mistake to let soiled tissues and other debris collect in dressing rooms that most women hate to use under the best circumstances. Even the best salesperson won't have much luck making multiple sales if the customer she's serving is anxious to get out of a messy little cubicle. Try making one employee responsible for a quick check of the dressing rooms several times each day.

Do your salespeople make the mistake of leading a shopper to the dressing room and then abandoning her until she emerges, ready to buy or leave the store? Since surveys by the score have shown that most women despise trying on clothing, your employees must make it as easy for them as possible. Train your help to linger near the fitting area, ready to do up buttons or close zippers. Make sure they offer to bring in other styles and sizes. A truly savvy salesperson will take careful note of the styles and sizes of garments the shopper selected to try. While the shopper is examining those garments, the good salesclerk will be off to the stockroom to find other pieces in the same size and mood. If a jacket, say, is one of the garments being tried, skirts, blouses, scarves, even hosiery should be brought for her consideration.

When a shopper enters your store is she ignored until she either asks for help or brings a selection to the cash register? A serious mistake. Everyone who comes in should be greeted cordially and asked, "Can I find something specific for you or would you prefer to look around?" If she replies, "I'm just looking," she should be told, "Fine, we're glad you came in. My name is Betty and I'm here to serve you when you're ready." You may want to lead her to a rack of dresses that you believe are her style. Or, if she indicates she wants to look at skirts, take her to where they are displayed and invite her to browse among them.

It's another mistake, however, to leave her alone too long. If you think she's interested in something and is shy about asking for help, offer once again to locate a specific size or color.

On the other hand, don't dog the heels of shoppers. If they say they want to look, permit them to do so freely. If you dash up every time a customer touches a garment, she'll probably feel badgered and leave.

When a dissatisfied customer comes in to return a garment, do you tell her something like, "Sorry, we don't accept returns"? If so, you're losing customers. Haven't you ever bought something and then decided it wasn't right after you got it home? You should at least have an exchange policy, to keep customers happy and shopping at your store.

Do your employees make a practice of brushing off irate customers by saying, "You'll have to speak to the manager"? That's a mistake that only makes the problem worse. No one is angry without having what she sees as a just reason. Therefore, she must be treated with sympathy from the outset. Make it a policy that all your employees will hear the entire complaint of any customer. Smile and nod in understanding while the customer tells her story. Really listen, too, so you don't have to stir up more anger by asking, in effect, what the woman has said. Don't belittle her complaint and don't push her off on someone else. Every person who works on the floor of your store should know how to try to resolve such difficulties at once. At the very least, write down (preferably on an official-looking printed form) all the details of the problem, including the customer's name, address, and phone number. Promise her you'll look into the problem and call her within 24 hours. Then do it. Even if you've been unable to gain approval to return her money, say, call her and explain. Stay in close touch with any complainant until the matter is resolved.

If your survey shows that you and your employees are making any mistakes like these, take immediate steps to correct them. Your customers will show their appreciation by spending more of their time and money in your store.